18 Minutes

18 MINUTES

Find Your Focus, Master Distraction, and
Get the Right Things Done

PETER BREGMAN

First published in the USA in 2011 by Business Plus

This edition published in Great Britain in 2011 by Orion

10 9 8 7 6 5 4 3 2 1

A CIP catalogue record for this book is available from the British Library.

ISBN: 9781409130574

Printed and bound by CPI Group (UK) Ltd, Croydon, CR0 4YY

The Orion Publishing Group Ltd
Orion House
5 Upper St Martin's Lane
London WC2H 9EA

An Hachette UK Company

The Orion Publishing Group's policy is to use papers that are natural, renewable and recyclable products and made from wood grown in sustainable forests. The logging and manufacturing processes are expected to conform to the environmental regulations of the country of origin.

This publication is designed to provide competent and reliable information regarding the subject matter covered. However, it is sold with the understanding that the author and publisher are not engaged in rendering legal, financial, or other professional advice. Laws and practices often vary from country to country and if legal, financial, or other expert assistance is required, the services of a professional should be sought. The author and publisher specifically disclaim any liability that is incurred from the use or application of the contents of this book.

To download an *18 Minutes* template and get other helpful resources go to www.peterbregman.com/18.

To my wife, Eleanor,
and my children, Isabelle, Sophia, and Daniel.
You inspire me to write.

Contents

Part Two: What Is This Year About?

Find Your Focus

Part Four: What Is This Moment About?
Mastering Distraction

18 MINUTES

INTRODUCTION

When Molly* arrived at work on the first day of her new job as the head of learning and development at a mid-size investment bank, she turned on her computer, logged in with the password they had given her, opened up her email program, and gasped.

She had been on the job less than a minute and there were already 385 messages in her inbox. It would take days to work through them, and by that time there would be hundreds more.

We start every day knowing we're not going to get it all done. And we look back on the years and wonder where they went and why we haven't accomplished what we had hoped.

Time is the only element in the world that is irretrievable

---

* Throughout the book, when a last name is not provided, the name and some details may have been changed.

when it's lost. Lose money and you can make more. Lose a friend and you can patch up the relationship. Lose a job and you can find another. But lose time and it's gone forever.

I have a friend, a rabbi named Hayyim Angel, who carries reading material with him whenever he goes to a meeting. Why? "Because," he told me, "according to the Talmud [the Jewish book of law], if someone comes late to a meeting they are committing the sin of stealing—stealing the time of the person who had to wait for them. And it's the worst kind of stealing because what was taken can never be returned. I don't want to cause anyone to sin. So I always make sure, if I have to wait for someone, they're never in a position of stealing my time."

And yet we steal time from ourselves constantly. Consider the following three stories...

Bill hadn't questioned the meeting his secretary had placed on his calendar. But now that he was in it—and bored—he wished he had. Bill pulled out his BlackBerry and began to read through his email. He was completely absorbed in his handheld when suddenly he heard Leticia, his boss, say his name. He looked up as Leticia continued, "What do you think we should do?" Bill had no idea what Leticia was referring to. *Where did that moment go?*

Rajit sat down with his laptop at nine o'clock on Wednesday morning knowing he had one thing he needed to do: write the proposal for a new client he was pitching in two days. But three phone calls, fifteen emails, two trips to the bathroom, thirty minutes buying plane tickets for a family vacation, and four impromptu conversations with employees later, he hadn't yet started it. And now his assistant just IM'd to remind him he had a lunch appointment in fifteen minutes. *Where did the day go?*

Marie walked into our twenty-fifth high school reunion and I was instantly reminded of her seventeen-year-old self. We sat down to talk, and she was all the things I remembered—beautiful, smart, talented, courageous, honest—with one exception. Her spark was gone. "I'm not unhappy," she told me. "I love my husband and children; my work is fine. In fact, my whole life is fine. But that's all it is: fine. I haven't really done anything. Every year I have plans but, well, stuff gets in the way." She feels the unexpressed potential inside her. She has things she wants to do. But somehow she doesn't make them happen. *Where did those years go?*

According to Newton's first law of motion, an object will continue moving at a constant velocity until an outside force acts upon it. What's true for objects is also true for people.

Either we keep moving along a path that isn't quite right but we fail to knock ourselves off it, or we intentionally choose the right path but keep getting knocked off it.

If we are to look back and feel good about what we've done—over a year, a day, or a moment—we need to break these patterns. To interrupt our inertia, everyday distractions, and gut responses. We need to intervene in our own lives.

Yet even if we know that, it's hard to do. It's not that Marie doesn't want a family. She does. And she wouldn't have it any other way. It's just that her role in her family has overwhelmed everything else in her life, so she looks back at the end of the year and asks herself where it went and why she's not thrilled. Still, she's not sure what to do differently next year.

Rajit had planned to write his proposal. But a number of forces lured him off his trajectory. Perhaps they were important distractions. But at the end of the day his proposal remained unwritten.

And Bill certainly hadn't intended to lose himself in his handheld; the email wasn't even that important. But his distraction became his focus and in the moment when his opinion was critical, all he could do was look up—at his boss—blankly.

18 Minutes provides a solution to these struggles and frustrations. It's a comprehensive approach to managing a year, a day, and a moment so that our lives move forward in a way that keeps us focused on, and doing, the things we decide are most important. An important first step in reclaiming our lives.

In part 1, *Pause*, you'll set the foundation that will enable you to take the insights from the book and translate them into action. In this part, I'll share some habits and mindsets that will position you to see possibilities beyond those you might otherwise notice. This part will help you focus on the right things, translate those things into a daily plan, follow through with that plan, and master the inevitable distractions that threaten to undermine your efforts.

In part 2, *What Is This Year About?*, you'll be guided to organize your life around the things that matter to you, make you happy, use your gifts, and move you toward your goals. In this part, I'll share four elements around which you should focus your efforts over the year. We'll look at some of the ways people tend to derail themselves from maintaining a clear focus, and I'll offer some strategies to avoid those derailers. In the final chapter of this section, you'll pull it all together to create your annual focus: the five areas where you want to spend the majority of your time over the next year.

In part 3, *What Is This Day About?*, you'll learn how to translate your annual focus into an 18-minute daily plan, ensuring that the *right* things get done, concretely structuring your day so it's productive, satisfying, and a measurable step toward fulfilling your focus for the year.

In part 4, *What Is This Moment About?*, you'll learn how to master distraction—sometimes by using it, sometimes by avoiding it. Here you'll learn how to get yourself motivated, how to follow through even when it's tempting to give up, and how to protect yourself and your time by creating the right kind of boundaries. This section is divided into three subsections—*Mastering Your Initiative, Mastering Your Boundaries,* and *Mastering Yourself*—and is full of simple tricks, tips, and rules to help you stay on track.

Finally, the conclusion, *Now What?*, sets you on your

way by sharing a foolproof method for gaining the critical momentum to move you in the direction you want to go.

There are many time management books out there that try to teach you how to get it *all* done. But that's a mistake. Because it's impossible to get it *all* done. And it's dangerous to try. You'll lose focus on what's important.

This book will help you make smart, thoughtful decisions about what's worth doing and what's not. And it will offer you some simple tools and skills to follow through on those decisions so you spend your time doing the things that matter while avoiding the things that don't. This book is also about enjoying the process. Managing your life shouldn't feel like a chore. And neither should reading a book about managing your life.

Standing in my apartment in New York City, I recently tapped the Google Earth app on my iPhone. Google Earth offers satellite maps of the entire world. When you first open the application, you see the whole earth, spinning in space, as though your cell phone screen were the window of a spaceship hovering above the earth's atmosphere. Then, slowly, it homes in on your location, and you feel like you're landing as the image becomes more clear and detailed. First you see your country, then your state, then your city, and eventually you are looking at the exact street where you're standing.

This time, though, when I tapped on the app, it opened in Savannah, Georgia, which must have been the last place I used it. So I tapped on the little circle in the bottom left corner—the FIND ME button—and Google Earth sent me back up into the air, shifted me to New York, and then landed me back on my street. Once there, it took a few seconds to settle in and focus.

Think of *18 Minutes* as the FIND ME button for your life. It will guide you to your most effective self. It will offer you a clear view of yourself and your surroundings, and then provide you with a map to help you get where you want to go. It's the app that can help you reclaim your life. Not simply based on where you've been or where others want you to be, but based on where you are now and where *you* want to go.

18 Minutes will home in on who you are and how you can best use your talents to achieve the things that will make you happy, productive, and successful. And if you are a little—or even a lot—out of focus, don't worry: *18 Minutes* will bring you back in.

I wrote this book so Molly, Bill, Rajit, Marie—and you— could look back at the end of each moment, each day, each year—and, when the time comes, life itself—and be able to say: "I used my time well."

PART ONE

Pause

Hover Above Your World

I started my business in 1998, out of a one-bedroom, fifth-floor walk-up apartment. My dream was to build a multimillion-dollar global management consulting firm filled with consultants, trainers, and coaches who would help people lead, manage, work, and live more successfully. A big dream.

Meanwhile, I had no clients and my company's only physical asset was a single computer. I survived on my savings for the first six months as I tried to build the business with little success. I didn't have enough work to sustain myself, let alone a team of consultants.

Then I won a large contract with a well-known investment bank. This was my big break, the project I could use to build my business. I needed to quickly assemble a team—six consultants at first and then, if all went according to plan, fifty more. I remember sitting in my two-hundred-square-foot living room/dining room/kitchen with Eleanor, my girlfriend, filled with the excitement of possibility and the trepidation of the test; could I pull this off?

I brought in an initial team who did a tremendous job meeting the client's expectations. Then, as the project expanded, so did the team. From New York to Chicago, San Francisco, Paris, London, Tokyo, and Hong Kong. And as the team expanded, so did my client base.

I had built my dream company in an unimaginably short period of time. It was everything I had hoped for, everything I had planned for.

That first year, I ended up making more money than I had in the previous three combined. The second year, I doubled that, and by the third year, I began to fantasize about retiring within the decade.

And yet, in the midst of all this success, I realized there was one thing I hadn't planned for: my happiness.

Somehow, I was missing that feeling of *I'm doing the right things with the right people in the right way to make the most of who I am*. At the time, I didn't know why and I was too busy to figure it out. Plus, everything seemed to be working just fine; why mess with success? So I kept doing what I was doing.

Then everything crashed; the dotcom revolution, the financial services industry, the demand for consulting, and, with it, my business.

By that time, Eleanor and I were married, Isabelle had been born, and we were in a tough spot. Bills were accumulating and my income was rapidly shrinking. I was stressed, but I also had a strange and quiet sense of relief. Now I began to fantasize, not of retiring, but of doing something else completely. Of reclaiming my life.

So I took acting classes, considered applying to medical school, actually applied to rabbinical school, started a phantom investment fund (with play money to see if I liked it, and if I was good at it), and continued to consult on my own. I was searching.

I slowed down my activity, reversed my forward momentum, paused before making choices, took more time off, and let my mind wander. I began to look more carefully at myself—at the world around me—and I began to notice hidden sides of me that felt unused, sub-optimized. I began to feel a growing power within me. A sense of untapped potential.

I wasn't yet sure what that potential was, but I was absolutely certain that it was worth cultivating. So I kept experimenting, kept noticing.

I had, in effect, pressed my FIND ME button. And when I did, I was thrown into the sky and offered a bird's-eye view of my world.

What I saw—what the pausing and the noticing and the recognizing enabled me to see—was that while I had gotten off track, I wasn't far off, and there was a safe way back down. I saw the path that would help me reclaim my life and allow me to bring my whole self into my work and my life. To spend my time on the things that mattered to me, the things I was good at, the things I enjoyed.

But I'm getting ahead of myself here. Because now, in part 1 of *18 Minutes*, you're about to be thrown into the air. You need that bird's-eye view. And to get it, you need to tap the FIND ME button, and then pause, as you let yourself fly high and hover above your world, preparing to land exactly where you want to be.

1

Slowing the Spin

Reducing Your Forward Momentum

I was moving as fast as I could and not getting anywhere, a feeling I'm well acquainted with. This time, though, it was deliberate: I was on a stationary bicycle.

When the towel draped over my handlebars fell to the ground, I tried to stop pedaling and get off. *Tried* being the operative word. I couldn't stop. There was simply too much forward momentum. The pedals seemed to be moving by a force of their own. It took me several moments of slowly backing off my speed before I could coax the pedals to stand still.

Momentum is hard to resist.

For example, fifteen minutes into a political argument with a friend, I realized I wasn't sure I agreed with my own position. But he was arguing so harshly that I found myself taking the opposite side, vehemently supporting ideas I didn't know enough about. And it was hard to stop.

It's especially hard to stop when you're invested in being

right, when you've spent time, energy, emotion, and sometimes money on your point of view.

I have several friends who got married and divorced
within a year or two. Every one of them told me they
knew, at the time they were getting married, that it
wouldn't work. But they had gone too far and they didn't
know how to stop it. It's the same story with people
I know who made some investments that seemed to be
going south. They knew things weren't working, but they
had already invested so much that it was hard to face the
mistake. In some cases, they put *more* money in and lost
it all.

Sometimes it's not so dramatic. It might be an argument
about which resources to put into which project. Or a decision about whether or not to continue to pursue a particular opportunity.

When you have the sense you've made a mistake but
you've already pushed so hard it would be embarrassing to
back out, how do you backpedal?

I have two strategies that help me pull back my own
momentum: Slow Down and Start Over.

1. **Slow down.** As I found on my stationary bike, it's
   almost impossible to backpedal hard enough to
   reverse direction on the spot. It helps to see it as a
   process. First, just stop pedaling so hard. Then, as
   the momentum starts to lose its force, gently begin to
   change direction.

   In a discussion in which you've been pushing

hard and suspect you might be wrong, begin to argue your point less and listen to the other side more. Buy some time by saying something like: "That's an interesting point; I need to think about it some more." Or, "Tell me more about what you mean." Listening is the perfect antidote to momentum since it doesn't commit you to any point of view.

If it's a financial investment you're unsure about, reduce it some without taking everything out, so that literally you have less invested in being right.

2. **Start over.** This is a mental game I learned from a friend who's a successful investor. I was hesitant to sell an investment that was doing poorly. My friend asked me the following question: If I were starting from scratch at today's price, would I purchase the investment? I sold it that day.

It's inevitable that our history impacts our current decisions. If I hired someone and invested energy and money supporting his success, it would be hard for me to admit he's not working out. But knowing what I know now, would I hire him? If not, I should let him go. Same thing with a project I've supported or a decision I've promoted. I imagine I'm a new manager coming into the project. Would I continue it? Invest additional resources? Or move on?

I've seen people's inability to admit they're wrong destroy their marriages and decimate their businesses and professional lives. In many cases, they tell me it's because they didn't want to appear weak. But it takes great strength of character to admit you're wrong or even to question your own views. And others perceive this as strength, too.

Great leaders have enough confidence to look critically at their own perspective and stay open to other people's points of view, using the technique of Slowing Down. Even when they know they're right.

Dr. Allan Rosenfield, past dean of Columbia's School of Public Health, was one such leader. He died in 2008 after spending more than four decades helping to shape the public health agenda, making a particularly huge impact on the lives of women and the lives of people with HIV. Columbia named its School of Public Health building in his honor.

I remember watching Allan in a conversation about whether children should be vaccinated, a public health issue about which he felt strongly and was clearly an expert. One of his friends, Lee, was arguing against vaccinations. Allan offered statistics on the millions of hospitalizations and deaths that have been averted in the past forty years because of vaccines for polio, mumps, measles, and so forth.

Lee then cited some research from an unnamed source on the Internet claiming that vaccines were doing more harm than good. Allan, one of the greatest public health experts of all time, would have been justified if he'd laughed. If he'd told Lee to get his information from more reliable, credible sources. If he'd repeated his arguments about the good that vaccines had done. But Allan didn't do any of that.

He simply looked at Lee, slowed down, and replied: "I haven't read that research. Send it to me. I'll look at it and let you know what I think."

Reducing your forward momentum is the first step to freeing yourself from the beliefs, habits, feelings, and busyness that may be limiting you.

2

The Girl Who Stopped Alligator Man

The Incredible Power of a Brief Pause

I am alligator man, a dangerous amphibious monster. I swim quietly toward my prey, a seven-year-old girl named Isabelle, who also happens to be my daughter. Sensing the danger, she nervously scans the surface of the pool. Suddenly she spots me. Our eyes lock for a brief moment. She smiles, screams, and lunges in the opposite direction, laughing. But I'm too fast. I push off the bottom of the pool and pounce. When I land within a few inches of her, she turns to face me, gasping, hand held up in the air.

"PAUSE!" she yells.

"What's the matter?"

"I swallowed water," she sputters.

So, of course, we pause.

Which gives me a few seconds to think: *Why don't we do that in real life?*

We've all hit the SEND button on an email and

immediately regretted it. So many of us do it regularly, in fact, that Google has added a feature to Gmail called UNDO SEND, which you can enable through Gmail settings. Once you hit SEND, Gmail holds the email for five seconds, during which time you can stop it from going out.

What's interesting is that, apparently, a five-second pause is all most people need to realize they've made a mistake.

With an email, hitting UNDO SEND can save a tremendous amount of time, energy, and backpedaling. But in real time—in person or on the phone—there's no such button. Sometimes, like a judge who tells the jury to ignore what a witness just said, we try to undo send. But once the words come out, there's no turning back. As my mother is fond of saying, "I forgive...but I don't forget."

The key, in real time, is to avoid the unproductive SEND in the first place.

Those five seconds Google gives us to undo our mistake? Maybe we can use them *before* we hit SEND. Perhaps that's all we need to avoid making the mistake. Five little seconds.

"Pause," Isabelle yelled when she swallowed the water. *Stop the action for a few seconds and let me catch my breath.*

There's no rule that says we need to respond to something right away. So pause. Take a few breaths.

One morning, due to a miscommunication about timing, I missed a meeting with Luigi, one of my clients. Later that day I was in the hallway in his office building when suddenly I heard him yell, "Hey Bregman, where were you?"

Immediately my heart rate shot up. Adrenaline flowed. And emotions flooded in. Embarrassment. Anger. Defensiveness. Who does Luigi think he is yelling across the hall at me like that in front of other people?

I spoke to Dr. Joshua Gordon, a neuroscientist and assistant professor at Columbia University, about my reaction. "There are direct pathways from sensory stimuli into the amygdala," he told me.

Come again?

"The amygdala is the emotional response center of the brain," he explained. "When something unsettling happens in the outside world, it immediately evokes an emotion."

That's fine. But pure, raw, unadulterated emotion is not the source of your best decisions. So how do you get beyond the emotion to rational thought?

It turns out while there's a war going on between you and someone else, there's another war going on in your brain between you and yourself. And that quiet internal battle is your prefrontal cortex trying to subdue your amygdala.

Think of the amygdala as the little red person in your head with the pitchfork saying, "I vote we clobber the guy!" and think of the prefrontal cortex as the little person dressed in white telling you, "Um, maybe it's not such a great idea to yell back. I mean, he is our client after all."

"The key is cognitive control of the amygdala by the

prefrontal cortex," Dr. Gordon told me. So I asked him how we could help our prefrontal cortex win the war. He paused for a minute and then answered, "If you take a breath and delay your action, you give the prefrontal cortex time to control the emotional response."

Why a breath? "Slowing down your breath has a direct calming effect on your brain."

"How long do we have to stall?" I asked. "How much time does our prefrontal cortex need to overcome our amygdala?"

"Not long. A second or two."

There we have it. Google's five seconds is a good rule of thumb. When Luigi yelled at me in the hall, I took a deep breath and gave my prefrontal cortex a little time to win. I knew there was a misunderstanding and I also knew my relationship with Luigi was important. So instead of yelling back, I walked over to him. It only took a few seconds. But that gave us both enough time to become reasonable.

Pause. Breathe. Then act. It turns out that Isabelle's reaction might be a good strategy for all of us.

"Ready?" I ask Isabelle once she seems to have recovered.

"Set, go!" she yells as she dives back into the water, clearly refreshed and focused on the stairs she's trying to reach.

I give her a five-second head start and then dive under the water after her.

A few seconds. That's all we need. To intentionally

choose the direction we want to move. To keep ourselves on track once we've started to move. And to periodically notice whether—after some time has passed—we're still moving in that right direction.

A brief pause will help you make a smarter next move.

3

The Day Andy Left Work Early

Stopping in Order to Speed Up

On a Friday afternoon almost twenty years ago, soon after I had started a job at a New York consulting firm, I was working on an important presentation with Dr. Andy Geller, who ran the office. We had promised to deliver it Monday morning, and we were running behind.

At two o'clock, Andy told me he had to leave.

"But we're not done," I stammered. Andy was not one to let work go unfinished, and neither was I.

"I know," he said, looking at his watch, "but it's Shabbat in a few hours and I need to get home. I'll come back Saturday night. If you can make it, too, we'll continue to work together then. Otherwise, do what you can the rest of today and tomorrow night I'll pick up where you left off." I decided to leave with him, and we met again at eight o'clock Saturday night. Refreshed and energetic, we finished our work together in record time.

A little backstory: Shabbat is the Jewish Sabbath; it starts at sundown on Friday and ends when it's dark Saturday night. The exact start time depends on sundown—it's earlier in the winter, later in the summer. For observant Jews, it's a rest day. No work, no travel, no computers or phones or TV. The way I heard it once, the idea is that for six days we exert our energy to change the world. On the seventh day the objective is simply to notice and enjoy the world exactly as it is without changing a thing.

Observant Jews spend Shabbat praying, eating, walking, and spending time with family and friends.

They're on to something.

This life is a marathon, not a sprint. In fact, each day is a marathon. Most of us don't go to work for twenty minutes a day, run as fast as we can, and then rest until the next race. We go to work early in the morning, run as fast as we can for eight, ten, twelve hours, then come home and run hard again with personal obligations and sometimes more work, before getting some sleep and doing it all over again.

That's why I'm such a fanatic about doing work you love. But even if you love it, that kind of schedule is deeply draining. Not an athlete in the world could sustain that schedule without rest. Most athletes have entire off seasons.

So if we're running a daily marathon, it might help to learn something from people who train for marathons.

Like my friend Amanda Kravat, who told me she was training to run the New York City Marathon. She'd never run anything before. I asked her how she planned to tackle this herculean feat with no experience.

"I'm simply going to follow the official marathon training plan," she said. I asked her to email it to me. Here's what I learned: If you want to run a marathon successfully without getting injured, spend four days a week doing short runs, one day a week running long and hard, and two days a week not running at all.

Now, that seems like a pretty smart schedule to me if you want to do *anything* challenging and sustain it over a long period of time. A few moderate days, one hard day, and a day or two of complete rest.

But how many of us work nonstop, day after day, without a break? It might feel like we're making progress, but that schedule will lead to injury for sure.

And when we do take the time to rest, we discover all sorts of things that help us perform better when we're working. Inevitably my best ideas come to me when I get away from my computer and go for a walk or run or simply engage in a casual conversation with a friend.

So one of the upsides to rest days is that they give you time to think. But there's also a downside, and it's serious enough that I believe it's the unconscious reason many of us resist taking them: *They give you time to think.*

My friend Hillary Small broke her foot and was confined to bed rest for several weeks. "The cast gave me a time-out card, which I never would have taken on my own," she told me, "and when I did slow down, I felt a deep sadness. I had nothing to distract me from the feeling that I had been living a life in which *my* needs were never a priority."

So it was hard for her. But it also gave her renewed energy to focus on her priorities. When we rest, we emerge stronger. There's a method of long-distance running that's becoming popular called the Run-Walk method; every few minutes of running is followed by a minute of walking. What's interesting is that people aren't just using this method to train, they're using it to race. And what's even more interesting is that they're beating their old run-the-entire-distance times.

Because slowing down, even for a few minutes here and there and even in the middle of a race, enables you to run faster and with better form. And, as a side benefit reported by Run-Walkers, it's a lot more fun.

Life, too, is a lot more fun when it's interspersed with some resting. A short walk in the middle of your race. A pause. A breath. A moment to take stock. To realign your form. Your focus. Your purpose.

I'm not talking about a stop as much as a ritual of self-imposed brief and strategic interruptions. A series of pauses to ask yourself a few important questions, to listen to the answers that arise, and to open yourself to making some changes—maybe big ones, maybe small ones—that will help you run strongly. That will ensure you're running the right race. And running it the right way. That will position you to win.

Faster, better, more fun? The only downside being time

to think? You don't have to believe in God to realize that slowing down is a good idea. But you do have to be religious about it.

> *Regular rest stops are useful interruptions. They will refuel your body and mind, naturally reorient your life toward what's important to you, and create the time and space to aim your efforts more accurately.*

4

Frostbite in the Spring

Seeing the World as It Is, Not as You Expect It to Be

At the very end of ski season, with the sun shining and little buds emerging from tree branches, I got frostbite while skiing. Not just a little frostbite; several of my toes were snow white. Thankfully I didn't lose any, but it took ten minutes in a hot shower for them to slowly and painfully return to their normal color.

Here's what's crazy: I ski all the time in the winter without getting frostbite, usually in temperatures well below freezing. So what happened?

Well, it turns out, it's precisely *because* it was spring that I got frostbite.

You see, in the winter, when it's cold, I wear a down jacket and several layers of thermal underwear. Most important, I use foot warmers—thin chemical packets that slide into my ski boots and emit heat for six hours. I need them because I have exceedingly wide feet and my boots are tight, which constricts my blood flow and makes me susceptible to frostbite when it's cold.

This time, since it was the very last ski weekend of spring, I wore a light jacket and didn't use my foot warmers.

Only the weather was below freezing. Twenty degrees to be exact.

Did I look at the temperature before I went out? Of course I did. I knew it was cold. My feet even started to hurt an hour into skiing, but I just kept on going. I simply ignored the data. Why? Because it was spring! I expected warmer weather. My past experience told me that this time of year was sunny and hot. Every other year at this time I skied in a T-shirt. And the previous weekend it was sixty degrees and I *did* ski in a T-shirt.

All of which overwhelmed the reality that, actually, it was cold enough to turn my toes white.

This was a good reminder of how easy it is to mistake our expectation for reality, the past for the present, and our desires for fact. And how painful it can be when we do.

There's a psychological term for this: *confirmation bias*. We look for the data, behaviors, and evidence that show us that things are the way we believe they should be. In other words, we look to confirm that we're right.

In the early 1990s, while working for a medium-size consulting firm, I went to Columbia University's executive MBA program. Two years after graduating, I was still working for the same firm, and I was ready for some new challenges. I had a number of new skills—skills the firm had, in part, paid for me to acquire—and I wanted to use them.

But the firm didn't see the new me. They saw the old me, the one they had hired and trained four years earlier. And so they continued to give me the same work and use me in the same ways they had before I earned my MBA.

Then a headhunter called and, since she hadn't known me before, she saw me as I was, not as she thought I should be. Within a few months, I'd left the firm and joined one that wanted to leverage my new skills.

Our inability—or unwillingness—to see things as they are is the cause of many personal, professional, and organizational failures. The world changes and yet we expect it to be the way we think it should be and so we don't take action.

I confront this challenge in my coaching all the time. The most challenging aspect of any coaching assignment isn't helping someone change—that's comparatively easy. The hard part is getting the people around the person to change their perception of him. Because once we form an opinion, we resist changing it.

Encyclopaedia Britannica, having built its two-hundred-year franchise selling massive books, was blindsided by digital media and had to scramble to compete in a changing world.

Why do we fall into the trap of being fooled by expectations?

Practice.

Usually our expectations are right. In the spring, it's warmer. People don't usually change drastically. And a two-hundred-year-old franchise is, well, two hundred years old. That's pretty solid.

Which makes us feel good. Safe. Right.

But sometimes we're wrong. Perhaps at one time we were right, and then things changed. But now, maybe, we're wrong and we don't like to admit that. We don't even see it. Because we're too busy looking for evidence to confirm our previous ideas.

Unfortunately, while confirmation bias makes us *feel* better, it makes us *behave* worse. So employees leave. Businesses falter. And I get frostbite.

How do we avoid falling into the trap of being fooled by expectations?

Practice.

Instead of looking for how things are the same, we can look for how they are different. Instead of seeking evidence to confirm our perspectives, we can seek to shake them up. Instead of wanting to be right, we can want to be wrong.

Of course, this takes a tremendous amount of confidence. Let's face it, we'd all prefer to be right rather than wrong.

But here's the irony: The more you look to be wrong, the more likely you'll end up right.

So next time you look at an employee, ask yourself: *What's changed?* Instead of focusing on what she's doing wrong, try looking for something new she does right that you never noticed before. Same thing for any relationship you're in.

And as you look at your industry, ask yourself how it's

changed and why that might mean your business strategy is off. Ask others to argue against you. Then listen instead of arguing.

Same goes for how you spend your time. Resist the temptation to accept the time-starved predicament you might be in. Do you *really* need to do everything you think you need to do?

Here's another great question to ask: *What do I not want to see?*

And next time you go outside, no matter the time of year, stick your hand out the window first and feel the temperature.

Because until you test your assumptions, you don't know for sure whether they're right. But once you question an assumption, once you open up to the possibility that things might not be the way they've always seemed, you need to be mentally prepared to be, well, wrong. Which is often a good thing. Because if you *are* wrong, it means there is a whole new set of possibilities open to you that you probably hadn't considered before.

The world changes—we change—faster than we tend to notice. To maximize your potential, you need to peer through the expectations that limit you and your choices. You need to see the world as it is—and yourself as you are.

5

Multiple Personalities Are Not a Disorder

Expanding Your View of Yourself

One evening, a woman sent an email to her father. Then she walked over to the window on the fourth floor of her office building, opened it, stepped through, and jumped to her death.

The email read: "I have decided to kill myself tonight... I can't take the new reorganization."

If this were an aberration, one depressed woman's inability to handle change, we could dismiss it. But dozens of employees of the same company have killed themselves. And many more than that have tried.

When confronted with this high rate of suicides, the management pointed out that, because of the company's size, the number wasn't statistically surprising. But there is something unusual happening, and not just at one company. According to America's Bureau of Labor Statistics, work-related suicides increased 28 percent between 2007 and 2008.

It's tempting to blame the companies. A good article in

The Economist pointed to a variety of things—the drive
for measurement and maximizing productivity, recession-
driven layoffs, poor management communication—that
contribute to a disheartening, depressing work environment. The article concludes that "companies need to do
more than pay lip service to the human side of management."
I agree. Certainly there are things leaders can and must
do to handle employees with more care, compassion, and
respect.

But the problem is deeper and more complicated than a
callous management team that cares about nothing except
profits.

The problem is also in us.

It's in how we see and define ourselves. It's in our identities.

The first question we ask when we meet people is inevitably, "What do you do?" We have become our work, our
professions. Connected 24/7 via BlackBerry, obsessively
checking email and voice mails, we have left no space for
other parts of ourselves.

If we spend all our time working, traveling to work,
planning to work, thinking about work, or communicat-
ing about work, then we will see ourselves as workers and
nothing more. As long as work is going well, we can survive that way.

But when we lose our jobs or our jobs are threatened,
then our very existence is put into question. "Establishing
your identity through work alone can restrict your sense
of self, and make you vulnerable to depression, loss of

self-worth, and loss of purpose when the work is threatened," Dr. Paul Rosenfield, assistant clinical professor of psychiatry at Columbia University, told me in a recent conversation.

Who am I if you take away my work? That's a question to which we'd better have a solid answer. And yet many of us don't. Fortunately, once we realize this we can do something about it.

We can diversify.

I don't mean diversifying your money, though that's a good idea, too. I mean diversifying your self. So that when one identity fails, the other ones keep you vibrant. If you lose your job but you identify passionately as a mother or a father, you'll be fine. If you have a strong religious identity or view yourself as an artist, you'll be fine. If you see yourself as an athlete, or even simply as a good, loyal friend, you'll be fine.

According to Dr. Rosenfield, this is an issue of mental health, even for the mentally ill. "People with mental illness often feel their identity is reduced to being mentally ill. Part of their recovery involves reclaiming other parts of their identity—being a friend, a volunteer, an artist, a dog lover, a student, a worker. It takes an active and bold effort to broaden and overcome the diminished sense of identity that results from dealing with mental illness, hospitalizations, medications, and one's doctors saying, 'You need to accept being mentally ill,' without also saying, 'But I believe you are more than your illness and you still have potential to do so many things in the world.'"

Here's the thing, though: It's not enough to see yourself in a certain way; you need to act on it. Build it into your year. Your day. It won't help if you identify as a father but rarely spend time with your children. Or if religion is a big part of your identity and yet you rarely engage in religious activities.

One obstacle is money. For many people, an obsession with work is really about having enough money to support themselves or their families. How can we work less and still survive?

Perhaps it's the only way to not only survive but thrive. Stepping away from your work might just be the key to increasing your productivity.

And having multiple identities will help you perform better in each one. Because you learn things as an athlete or a parent or a poet that will make you a better employee or leader or friend. So the more you invest yourself in multiple identities, the less likely it is that you'll lose any one of them.

Of course, if you do lose one, you'll be okay because you've got the others.

It's useful to question the basic assumptions you have about yourself. Even the ones as ingrained as *Who am I?* or, perhaps more accurately, *Who are we?* Because, most likely, you'll find all sorts of people living in you—people you never fully appreciated were there. And those underappreciated aspects of yourself may turn out to be the keys to focusing on the right things—and getting them done. Seeing yourself fully, broadly, and clearly is crucial.

And if you still believe that doing nothing but work is necessary to support your lifestyle, then it's worth looking at ways to moderate your lifestyle so you don't kill yourself trying to maintain it.

Walk away from the email and have dinner with your family. Leave work at a decent hour and play tennis with a friend. Choose rituals that have meaning to you and do them religiously. Most important, be consistent—doing the same thing repeatedly over time solidifies your identity.

A good friend of mine lost her job about a year ago, and I called at the time to see if I could do anything. My intention was to help her find a new job as soon as possible; I knew money was tight.

I was pleasantly surprised, though. She told me she had decided to postpone her job search for a few months. She was pregnant and wanted to focus on that for a while. Once she felt ready, she would look for work. She was too busy creating an identity as a mother to get caught up in her identity as a worker.

Eventually I received an email from her telling me she was back at work. "I love the job," she told me. "It's a great balance to motherhood."

> *Life isn't just about some of you; it's about all of you.*
> *Don't negate, integrate.*

6

Why We're Fascinated with Susan Boyle

Recognizing Your Own Potential

Susan Boyle, who performed on the U.K. television show *Britain's Got Talent*, captured the world's attention.

In case you missed it, she was a forty-seven-year-old unemployed charity worker who lived with her cat in a small village in Scotland.

As soon as she walked on stage, the audience began to snicker and roll their eyes. Simon Cowell, the show's host, asked her some pre-performance questions in his famously condescending style, and to the audience's enjoyment she answered awkwardly.

She was painfully ordinary, and everyone was prepared, looking forward even, to see her fail.

By now, if you don't know the story, you can guess it, right? She more than wowed them. She opened her mouth to sing, and, as judge Piers Morgan later said, she had "the voice of an angel."

She wasn't painfully ordinary; she was amazingly extraordinary. The audience immediately jumped to a standing ovation and stayed there until the end of the song. A week after she performed, the YouTube video of Susan's performance had received more than thirty-five million views.

We were riveted, and an article in *USA Today* did a good job of cataloging all the reasons. We prejudged her by her looks and were fooled. We experienced the gamut of emotions in a few short moments: guilt, shame, vindication, hope. She's a modern-day Cinderella, and these days, it's a wonderful distraction and inspiration to witness the triumph of the human spirit.

But there's something else Susan Boyle awakens in us as we watch her come out of her shell: our own selves. Who among us does not move through life with the hidden sense, maybe even quiet desperation, that we are destined for more? That underneath our ordinary exterior lies an extraordinary soul? That given the right opportunity, the right stage, the right audience, we would shine as the stars we truly are?

That promise underlies most successful advertising campaigns: the desire to transform from caterpillar to butterfly. Maybe if you buy that [fill in the blank], people will see you for the sophisticated, cool, gorgeous, talented, lovable person you know you really are.

But in our less desperate moments, we know we can't purchase that transformation. Although Susan Boyle became an overnight sensation, hers was not an overnight transformation. She's been practicing singing since she was twelve. In her case, overnight was thirty-five years.

It's easy to admire Susan. But it's far more interesting to be transformed by her. "There is grace," a friend once wrote to me, "in being molded by your own gifts."

To allow yourself to be molded by your own gifts takes courage. You have to be willing to stand there, exposed and authentic, while the audience rolls their eyes at you and sneers, expecting failure. And then, of course, you have to fail, laugh or cry, and keep going until, one day, they stop laughing and start clapping.

But you can't do it alone. Susan Boyle didn't; she had a voice coach, Fred O'Neil, who worked with her for years and encouraged her to audition. And she had her mother.

"She was the one who said I should enter *Britain's Got Talent*. We used to watch it together," Boyle told the British paper *The Times* of her mother, who died in 2007. "She thought I would win....I am doing it as a tribute to my mum, and I think she would be very proud."

If we're lucky, we have parents who encourage us. Nothing really replaces a mother or father who believes in you. But even if you don't have parents who believe in you, it's important to have someone. Someone you trust enough that when they offer criticism, you know it's to draw you out more fully, not shut you down even partially.

And a good supporting friend even sees through the talent, right through to you. With her mother gone, Boyle still has O'Neil. As he said to *The Telegraph*, he was worried all this attention was obscuring "the real person" he knew.

"I am concerned about her being surrounded by all

these PR people," he said, "that she will not be given the time to sing."

Susan Boyle is a phenomenal role model for all of us, not just because of her talent or her courage or her perseverance or her supportive friends. She is a phenomenal role model for us because she is us, in all our awkward ordinariness and amazing extraordinariness.

> *Don't settle for being less than you are. It won't serve others and it won't serve you.*

7

You Don't Have to Like Him

Where Do You Want to Land?

Several years ago, I took on a new client in New York City. This company had lawsuits against it, high turnover, and terrible press. One of the first people I met was Hunter, a senior leader.

"Look, Peter, you seem like a nice guy," Hunter said with a smile as he looked at me from across his desk, "but there have been several consultants before you and there will be several more after you. If you think you're going to change the way we do things here, well, you're mistaken."

Hunter smiled at me again, and I had a strong, visceral reaction—I immediately disliked him.

After leaving the meeting, I called my uncle, a successful businessman in London, and told him the story. "I can't work with this company."

"Why not?" my uncle asked.

"Honestly? I really don't like the guy," I answered.

He laughed. "You don't have to like him, Peter. You just have to do business with him."

My uncle was right. And he was pointing out a habit that costs many of us tremendous opportunity. Our reaction to an event creates an unproductive outcome.

event → reaction → **outcome**

In my case, the *event* was that Hunter told me I wouldn't be effective. My *reaction* was to dislike Hunter and avoid working with him. The *outcome* would have been the loss of that client.

This simple event-reaction-outcome chain governs most of our spontaneous action. Something or someone hooks us and we react. Someone yells at us, we yell back and create the outcome of a damaged relationship. It's not that we *want* a damaged relationship; it's just what *happens* when we yell back.

And that's the problem. The most important part of the chain, arguably the only part that really matters, the *outcome*, is collateral damage from our reaction. It's not intentional. We're reacting to the *event*. The *outcome* is simply fallout.

But this time, before making that mistake, I paused, which gave my rational self time to negotiate with my emotional self. And luckily for me, during that negotiation, they must have agreed to call my uncle for advice.

My uncle offered an alternative chain. Focus on the outcome, then choose your reaction.

event → **outcome** → reaction

Rather than focus on my personal reaction to Hunter, my uncle suggested that I focus on what I wanted, which was to grow the business.

When an unsettling event occurs, pause before reacting. In that pause, ask yourself a single question: *What is the outcome I want?* Then, instead of reacting to the *event*, react to the *outcome*.

In other words, stop reacting to the past and start reacting to the future.

If someone yells at you, pause before yelling back. Then ask yourself what outcome you want. If the answer is "An improved relationship," don't yell back. Instead, in a normal voice, empathize with their anger and ask some questions about the concerns raised in the midst of the screaming. That's a reaction that will achieve a better relationship.

Here's the hard part: You react to the event because it's asking you to react to it. But just because the event *catalyzed* your action doesn't mean it should *determine* it. How you react can and should be determined by the outcome—by the future you want to create.

Maybe a colleague comes to you complaining about a situation she's in with her boss (event). How should you respond (reaction)? If the outcome you want is for her to feel supported, then listen with empathy. If you want to help her, then offer solutions. If you simply want to get back to work, then find a graceful escape.

This is particularly useful in personal relationships.

When a problem is presented to me (event), my instinct is to solve it (reaction). On the other hand, what I want most with my wife, Eleanor, is a strong vibrant relationship (outcome). So when she comes to me with a problem, instead of immediately trying to solve it, I ask her what she wants me to do. Listen? Solve? Coach? I am surprised, disappointed even, by the number of times she says, "Just listen." *Wait*, I want to tell her, *I have ideas. Solutions! I can help.* But after more than ten years of marriage, I've realized that listening is sometimes all the help she wants from me. So I listen.

In the end, I continued to work with Hunter and his company for several years. Instead of focusing on Hunter, I focused on the goal of creating a more functional, productive management process for the company.

At one point, I was back in Hunter's office, planning an offsite I was going to lead for him, when I saw my book on his bookshelf.

"Have you read it?" I asked.

"Yes," he answered, "and it's not bad."

You know, I thought, *I might like this guy after all.*

Not that it matters.

Knowing what outcome you want will enable you to focus on what matters and escape the whirlwind of activity that too often leads nowhere fast.

Where We Are

Slow down your momentum. Pause in the moment. Stop to reset. Look around—beyond what you expect things to be—to see things as they really are. Expand your view of yourself. Be open to your extraordinary potential. Focus on your outcome.

These behaviors—steps really—will help you see yourself, and the world, plainly and distinctly. They'll send you up in the air to see what's below more clearly. They'll help you cut through your—and other people's—unhelpful biases, preconceptions, and dead-end ruts. They'll help you experiment and tap deeply into resources you may have forgotten were there. And they'll guide you to draw from your bottomless well of talent to achieve concrete things in the world.

What particular things? What specific talent? That's the focus of part 2.

PART TWO

What Is This Year About?

Find Your Focus

In the introduction to part 1, I shared the first part of my story. How I built the company I had dreamed of creating and then, when it all crashed, I pressed the FIND ME button and hovered over my world, pausing and noticing. I experimented; I explored acting, medical school, rabbinical school, and investment management.

And as I experimented, I began to descend back to earth, but in a slightly different location. Not a different country, but a different city. Or maybe just a different street in the same city.

Here's what I noticed: While ultimately, I didn't want to be an actor, rabbi, doctor, or investment manager, there were things about each of those roles that were attractive to me. I wanted to be playful, express myself, and experiment. I wanted to be useful and help others in a hands-on way. I wanted to have, and express, meaning and depth in my work. I wanted to be inspired and to inspire others. And I wanted to make good money.

I also noticed that I really liked—and wanted to continue—consulting. I loved the client partnerships and relationships I developed. I thoroughly enjoyed—and was good at—looking at problems and devising creative solutions to address them. I had a passion for ideas of all sorts, and it made me happy to use them to help people make changes in their companies and in their lives. I loved thinking and writing and speaking in ways that inspired others.

What I didn't like was running a consulting company, which to me often felt like the opposite of consulting. Instead of inventing innovative customized solutions to a particular problem, I had to create standardized methods that I could replicate across all my consultants around the world. Instead of spending my time with clients, I was spending my time managing other consultants. Instead of thinking up new ideas or writing or speaking, I was spending my time running, and growing, the business.

What I realized—my big *aha*—was that I could have it all. If I consulted in a certain way, I could combine what attracted me about being an actor, doctor, rabbi, and investment manager into one. I could be a playful, expressive, experimental, useful, hands-on, meaningful, deep, inspiring consultant (who made good money). And it would be the perfect job for me since I would be leveraging my strengths, embracing my weaknesses, asserting my differences, and pursuing my passions.

That, I discovered, was my way back down to earth. Not

just to financial or career success, but to happiness and ful-fillment, because it would allow me—force me, actually—to bring my whole self into my work and my life. To spend my time on the things that are important to me. The things that make me different, that make me matter.

Still, as I began to practice consulting in my own, new way, it wasn't always easy. I made mistakes. I failed repeatedly. Sometimes, when one part of my plan wasn't working, I questioned the whole plan. Other times, I became so focused on doing things a certain way that I missed great opportunities around me. And periodically, when I didn't know what to do, I froze and didn't do anything.

Those are pitfalls that you may or may not avoid, but knowing about them ahead of time will help you move through them as you find your focus.

So often we scramble to get a lot accomplished in a day, and succeed—only to realize, in retrospect, that those things we accomplished won't get us where we want to go. It's not a lack of effort. It's a lack of direction and focus.

In order to reclaim your life, first you need to focus on what your life is all about. Otherwise, no matter how hard you work, you'll just be frittering your time away. As you design a plan for where you want to spend your time over the next year, the chapters in this next section will help you find that focus. They'll help you take a broader, more open, thoughtful perspective in your work and in your life. They'll help you create a plan that reflects your full potential. And they'll nudge you, gently coaxing that potential out of you and into the world.

We'll look at the four elements—your strengths, weaknesses, differences, and passions—that form the foundation of your success and happiness. It's at the intersection of those four elements that your time will be best spent. Along the way, we'll explore some of the pitfalls to avoid—possible left or right turns that might send you off in the wrong direction. Finally, in the last chapter, you'll define the annual focus that will serve as the basis for all your daily plans. So that you spend your time where it matters most.

8

What to Do When You Don't Know What to Do

Choosing Your Next Move at the Intersection of the Four Elements

I was on my way to Princeton University, where I was a student more than twenty years ago, to give a speech about life after college. As I traveled to the campus, I remembered a single question that haunted my last few months of schooling: *Now what?*

I had no good answer. I didn't have a job. I didn't have a plan.

Which, as it turns out, might have been a pretty good plan after all.

Mark Zuckerberg and his college roommates were computer science students without any real plan. They started Facebook because it was fun, used their talents, and was a novel way for Harvard students and alumni to stay in touch. Zuckerberg never anticipated it would host more than four hundred million members. And he had no clear idea where the money would come from. But he kept at it until, in 2007, Facebook let outside developers create applications for it, and game developers started buying ads on Facebook to keep attracting players. Hardly Zuckerberg's strategy in 2004.

Similarly, when Larry Page and Sergey Brin, founders of Google, started writing code in 1996, they had no clear plan or idea how they would make money. But that didn't stop them from starting. It wasn't until 2002 and 2003 that AdWords and AdSense became the company's money-making platform.

In a few chapters, I'll address the importance of staying flexible and the dangers of sticking too closely to your plan. But what if you have no plan?

That's the situation so many of us face—not just when we graduate but throughout our lives. Even those who grew up in the generation that stayed with a company thirty years are now, thankfully, living long enough to have second and third careers. And the younger generation is switching jobs every few years, often changing careers entirely. My yoga teacher used to be a casting director. Yesterday's plan may not apply today.

The limitless options we encounter make it difficult to create a plan. In a study led by Sheena Iyengar, a management professor at Columbia University Business School, one group of people was presented with samples of six different jams available for purchase while another group was presented with twenty-four different jams. The twenty-four-jam group showed much greater interest when sampling, but the six-jam group was ten times more likely to actually purchase a jam. We're ten times more likely to take action when choice is limited!

It's easy to become paralyzed when so many choices exist. We can't decide among them so we end up not choosing.

But life goes on, and no choice becomes the de facto choice, and suddenly we look back and feel like our talents have been wasted. We leave the store without buying any jam at all.

We need a way to get started *now*, to move in the right direction, even when we don't have a plan.

So what makes people like Mark Zuckerberg, Larry Page, and Sergey Brin so successful? Some of it is opportunity. Some of it is persistence. And some is sheer luck. But there's another set of ingredients that encourages opportunity, persistence, and luck. I call them the four elements. The four behaviors around which you should shape your next year:

1. Leverage your strengths.
2. Embrace your weaknesses.
3. Assert your differences.
4. Pursue your passions.

Zuckerberg, Page, and Brin loved technology and were great with it. None of them operated alone—they partnered with people to complement their weaknesses. And in style as well as substance, they offered unique approaches that differentiated them and their companies from anything else out there.

For me, at Princeton, it was outdoor leadership. My strength was group dynamics. My weakness—a neurotic safety consciousness—was an asset in this situation. I loved being with others in the outdoors. And having grown up in New York City, my urban outlook brought a unique perspective to teaching people who were also new to the outdoors.

Still, I had no idea how I was supposed to turn any of that into gainful employment. I couldn't see how it would provide a career for me in the long term. I couldn't see raising a family while living in the woods. It was far from perfect. So I almost threw it all out. I almost went to law school.

But I didn't. Instead, I chose to stick with what I was doing, experimenting to improve my focus on the four elements while changing those things that detracted from them.

One thing I experimented with was doing outdoor team building with corporate groups. I could do that while living a more stable life. And it leveraged my differences even more—I knew more about the corporate world than most others in outdoor leadership.

So I started a company. One decision led to another. Eighteen years later, I'm still changing my business, morphing it to take better advantage of my strengths, weaknesses, differences, and passions. What will it look like in three years? I'm not sure.

The entire path need not be clear. Most successful people and businesses have meandered their way to success by exercising their talents in ways they never would have imagined at the outset.

Here's what's fortunate: You're already doing something—whether it's a job, a hobby, or an occasional recreational pastime—that exploits your strengths, allows for your weaknesses, uses your differences, and excites your passion. All you have to do is notice it.

The speech I gave when I arrived at Princeton? The guidance I could offer the students who were worrying about their futures? Forget about your future. For just a moment, stop fixating on where you want to go. Instead, focus on where you are. Spend some time understanding *who* you are. And start from there.

Start experimenting from who you are and choose your next move—your focus for the year—at the intersection of the four elements. That's where your power lies.

9

Reinvent the Game

Element One: Leverage Your Strengths

How can a few pirates in small boats capture and hold huge tanker ships hostage? How can a few scattered people in caves halfway across the world instill fear in the hearts of millions of citizens in the largest, most powerful countries in the world? How can a single independent contractor beat out a thirty-thousand-person consulting firm to win a multimillion-dollar contract?

In *A Separate Peace*, John Knowles's coming-of-age novel, Phineas invents the game Blitzball, in which everyone chases a single ball carrier, who must outrun every other competitor. As it happens, Phineas always wins because the rules of the game—a game he invented—favor his particular skills.

That's the secret of the successful underdog. Play the game you know you can win, even if it means inventing it yourself.

Entrepreneurs intuitively understand this; they start

their own companies for exactly this reason. I know a tremendous number of extremely successful people who could never get a job in a corporation because they never went to college. So they started their own companies: companies they designed to play to their unique strengths. They invented a game they could win, and then they played it.

In his book *Moneyball*, Michael Lewis explains how the Oakland A's, with $41 million in salaries, consistently beat teams with more than $100 million in salaries. The richer teams hired the top players based on the traditional criteria: the highest batting averages, most bases stolen, most hits that brought a runner home, and—get this—the all-American look.

Other poorer teams who used the same criteria as the rich ones had to settle for second- or third-tier people who were less expensive. Which basically guaranteed that the richest teams had the best players and won.

But the Oakland A's studied the game and reinvented the rules. They realized that the number of times a player got on a base (on-base percentage) combined with the number of bases a player got each time he came to bat (slugging percentage) was a better predictor of success. And since no other teams were looking at those particular criteria, the players who excelled in those areas were relatively cheap to sign. Hiring those people was a game the Oakland A's could win.

Large consulting firms spend tens of thousands of dollars on glossy proposals to clients. But is that what wins the game? Perhaps what really wins is client ownership over the project, and if you sit with the client and design the project with her, your one-page proposal (that she, in effect, co-wrote with you) will beat their hundred pages every time—at a fraction of the cost. That's a game an independent contractor can win.

Malcolm Gladwell, in his *New Yorker* article "How David Beats Goliath," talks about the moment that David shed his armor. He knew he couldn't win a game of strength against strength. But he also knew he was faster, more agile, and had better aim. So he picked up five stones, dashed out of the pack, and won the battle. He broke the rules and reinvented the game.

Gladwell refers to research done by the political scientist Ivan Arreguin-Toft, who looked at every war fought in the past two hundred years in which one side was at least *ten times stronger* than the other. He found that the weaker side won almost 30 percent of the time—a remarkable feat. The reason? They fought a different war than their opponents.

The 70 percent that lost? They fought the conventional way; they engaged in battle using the same rules as their stronger opponents.

In 1981, Doug Lenat, a computer scientist, entered a war game tournament in which each contestant was given a fictional trillion-dollar budget to spend on a naval fleet of their choosing. The other contenders had deep military backgrounds and built a conventional naval fleet with boats of various sizes with strong defenses.

But Lenat had no military background. He simply fed the rules of the tournament to a computer program he invented: a program that was built to win, not to follow convention.

"The program came up with a strategy of spending the trillion dollars on an astronomical number of small ships like P.T. boats, with powerful weapons but absolutely no defense and no mobility," Lenat said. "They just sat there. Basically if they were hit once, they would sink. And what happened is that the enemy would take its shots and every one of those shots would sink our ships. But it didn't matter, because we had so many."

Lenat won the game in a landslide.

What game are you playing? Is it the right game for your particular skills and talents? Is it a perfect setup for you or your company to win? If not, then perhaps it's time to play a different game or invent one of your own: one you can win.

> *The first element is your strengths. Over the coming year, play the game that is perfectly suited to your strengths.*

10

I'll Just Take the Shrimp

Element Two: Embrace Your Weaknesses

I was having lunch with a friend of mine, Geoff, a man who has been very successful in business. Deeply generous, he gave away the majority of his fortune, hundreds of millions of dollars, to a foundation.

When the waiter came to take our order, Geoff asked for the Caesar salad with shrimp and then added, "But instead of shrimp, could you put salmon on the salad?"

"That's no problem, sir," the waiter responded. "Just so you know, though, it'll be an extra dollar."

"You know," Geoff replied after a moment's hesitation, "forget it. I'll just take the shrimp."

What do you call that? Cheap? Strange? Dysfunctional? I call it the secret to his success. Not yours, by the way. His.

Geoff has a fixation on value. He can't stand the idea of spending a single extra dollar if it doesn't provide at least two dollars of value. Maybe that's extreme. But so is a fortune (and foundation) of hundreds of millions of dollars. He's not successful *despite* his quirk; he's successful *because* of it.

And what's made Geoff successful is that he's not embarrassed about it. Or ashamed. He doesn't hide or repress or deny it.

He uses it.

I was talking to a famous guy I know—someone whose name you would instantly recognize—when he started name-dropping. *Hold on,* I thought, *you don't have to name-drop to me. I'm already impressed. In fact, you're the name I use when I'm name-dropping.*

Why was my famous friend name-dropping? Because after everything he's achieved, he's still insecure. Which is, at least in part, why he's achieved so much. He never would have worked so hard, spent so much time and effort on his projects, continued to apply himself after he had "made it," if he weren't insecure. His dysfunction has turned out to be tremendously functional.

"The most interesting novels," *Newsweek* editor Malcolm Jones wrote in a recent book review, "are the ones where the flaws and virtues can't be pulled apart."

That's even truer for people. The most powerful ones don't conquer their dysfunctions, quirks, and potentially embarrassing insecurities. They seamlessly integrate them to make an impact in the world.

Another man I know was the driving force behind health reforms that saved the lives of millions of people in the developing world. Literally millions. Certainly he achieved this feat with great strengths. He was deeply connected with his values. He worked tirelessly and with single-minded focus. He cared deeply about others, friends and strangers alike, and did whatever he could to help them.

But he had a quirk. He lived and worked in the hyper-intellectual world of academia, where nuance is valued far above simplicity. Success as an academic traditionally lies in one's ability to see and expound the gray.

But he never saw the gray. He saw the world in black and white, right and wrong. This simplistic view of the world is something that people in academia try to hide or overcome all the time. But he never hid his simplicity. He embraced it. And that was the source of his power, the secret ingredient that enabled him to save so many lives. He cut through the morass of a debate and arrived at the simplicity of righteous action.

Yet another friend, an outstanding investment manager, spends all his time obsessively looking at, thinking about, and reading financial statements of companies in which he is considering investing. He lives and breathes them. I once invited him to spend the weekend skiing. Instead of skis, he brought a stack of annual reports that stood three feet high. That's just weird. But his obsession has made him one of the best stock pickers in the world.

We all have quirks and obsessions like these. Maybe we don't admit them, even to ourselves. Or we worry that they detract from our success and work hard to train ourselves out of them.

But that's a mistake. Our quirks very well may be the secret to our power.

> *The second element is your weaknesses. Rather than avoid them, embrace your weaknesses and spend your time this year where they're an asset instead of a liability.*

11

Heated Seats

Element Three: Assert Your Differences

I was running along the six-mile loop in Central Park on a cold winter day when I passed the southernmost end of the park and noticed a large number of miserable-looking pedicab drivers huddled together to keep warm. Periodically, one reached out to a passing pedestrian, but no one seemed to want a ride in a bicycle-drawn carriage. It was too cold.

And then, to my surprise, a little farther along the run I saw a pedicab—with passengers in it—circling the park. The reason this pedicab had been hired instead of the others was immediately obvious. On both sides of his small carriage hung signs with large letters that read HEATED SEATS.

In any highly competitive field—and these days every field is highly competitive—being different is the only way to win. Nobody wants to sell a commodity, and nobody wants to be a commodity.

Yet even though we all know that, most of us spend a tremendous amount of effort trying *not* to be different. We model ourselves and our businesses after other successful people and businesses, spending considerable money and energy discovering and replicating best practices, looking for that one recipe for success.

Here's the thing: If you look like other people, and if your business looks like other businesses, then all you've done is increase your pool of competition.

I was consulting with American Express in 1993 when Harvey Golub became the new CEO. He wore suspenders. Within a few weeks, so did everyone else. In our corporate cultures, we school, like fish. We try especially hard to fit in when we worry about getting laid off. Maybe, we think, standing out will remind them that we're here, and then they'll lay us off, too.

But fitting in has the opposite effect. It makes you dispensable. If you're like everyone else, then how critical to the business can you be?

That's how my friend Paul lost his job. He was very successful at fitting in. It was the early 1990s and he was a partner at his consulting firm. He was a good consultant—I learned a lot from him—and for a long time he acted like the other partners. He sold the projects they sold. Billed the hours they billed.

Then, in a year and a half, Paul's mother died, his brother died, and he got divorced. He couldn't keep up his sales or his billable hours. And here's the important part: He didn't bring anything unique to the table beyond those things. It wasn't that he couldn't, as we'll see in a moment. But he didn't. So he lost his job.

Trying to distinguish ourselves by being the same as others, only better, is hard to do and even harder to sustain. There are too many smart, hardworking people out there all trying to excel by being the best at what everyone else is doing.

It's simply easier to be different.

Entertainment is a great example. In a field with a tremendous number of beautiful, sexy, talented people, what are the chances that you'll be noticed by being even more beautiful, sexy, and talented? But Susan Boyle was different. She broke the mold. Which is why her YouTube videos received *more than one hundred million hits*. If she looked like every other aspiring singer, would the world have noticed?

If you're seventy, don't get a face-lift and pretend to be thirty. Embrace seventy and use it to your advantage. According to a tremendous body of research, talent is not inborn, it's created by practice. Which gives a seventy-year-old a tremendous advantage over a thirty-year-old.

But even in our diversity-focused corporations, it's hard to be different because we have cultural norms that encourage sameness. That's why we have dress codes. And expressions like "Don't rock the boat." My advice? Rock on.

That's what Paul eventually did. After he lost his job, Paul realized that he was never fully himself as a partner in his consulting firm. He had more to offer. He wanted to connect more deeply with his clients, help them achieve things outside of their working lives, and engage with them on issues beyond the bottom line.

Now his name is Paramacharya Swami Parameshwarananda (you can call him Swamiji for short). He is the resident spiritual master at an ashram in Colorado. His change might seem drastic, but it was easy for him because each step he took was a step toward himself. And now he couldn't be happier or more effective. He serves on various boards and leadership councils and is a driving force behind several educational and humanitarian projects around the world.

He's still doing many of the same things he did as a failed consultant in New Jersey, but he's more successful because he feels and acts like himself. In his words, "I'm living my inner truth." And he is indispensable. Not simply for what he does, but for who he is.

Now, I'm not suggesting you go live in an ashram in Colorado. For most people that would be absurd. And copying someone else who's different won't help. You'll never be as good a version of someone else as you are of yourself.

How can you move closer to contributing your unique value? What are your "heated seats"? Can you be more effective by being more yourself?

Face it: You're different. And the sooner you appreciate it, the sooner you embrace and assert it, the more successful you'll be. The same goes for your business.

That's why one pedicab driver with heated seats can

stay busy all day while the others huddle around, fareless, trying to stay warm.

> *The third element is your differences. Assert them. Don't waste your year, and your competitive advantage, trying to blend in.*

12

The Pilot Who Saved 155 Passengers

Element Four: Pursue Your Passion (Desire)

Captain Greg Davis is an outstanding fishing guide. I went out with him early one morning off the coast of Savannah, Georgia, and came back a few hours later with several fish so big that I needed help just holding them up. Most other guides came back that morning with nothing.

What makes Greg such a remarkable guide? If you were hiring guides, could you predict he would be a star?

Wouldn't it be great if we could predict the areas where we would be most likely to shine? Where we would be stars? What if we could predict which song we should sing—and on which stage—to truly reveal our inner Susan Boyle? Well, we can.

On January 15, 2009, Captain C. B. Sullenberger made an emergency landing of his fifty-ton passenger aircraft, softly gliding it onto the Hudson River in New York City, saving the lives of all 155 people on board. Miraculous? Or predictable?

What do we know about Captain Sullenberger? Before the landing that exposed his particular brilliance, could you have predicted he would have the skill, the presence, the leadership to become the star that he is today?

Earlier in my career, I spent four years working in a management consulting company creating models to use in hiring people. Our clients, mostly large, public companies, spent hundreds of thousands of dollars on research we performed in their companies to predict who would be a star performer.

Here was our process: We interviewed both star and average performers in a client company and identified the characteristics that distinguished the stars from the rest. Then we helped the company interview people and hire the ones who fit the model.

Sounds reasonable. But it's not. It's tremendously expensive and time consuming. It requires intensive interviews that demand a great deal of skill; it's only as effective as the person doing the interviewing and hiring. And even if you have the money, time, and skill, you end up hiring past stars, not future ones.

Some would argue that the only thing that predicts success in a job is actual success in that job. That's why financial services firms hire close to ten times the number of analysts they need and then, a year or two later, keep the ones who succeed and let the others go. Of course, that's even more expensive and time consuming than our modeling process.

There is a much cheaper, easier way to place a person—
you or anyone—in a position to succeed. Ask one question:

What do you do in your spare time?

In Captain Sullenberger's case, the first clue that he
would become Captain Sullenberger the hero is that, in his
teens, when most of his friends were getting their driver's
licenses, he got his pilot's license. What did he do for fun?
He flew glider planes, which is basically what he did when
he landed in the Hudson River with no engines. Extracur-
ricular activities? He was an accident investigator for the Air
Line Pilots Association and worked with federal aviation
officials to improve training and methods for evacuating
aircraft in emergencies.

As a boy, he built model aircraft carriers with tiny planes
on them, careful to paint every last piece. Perhaps that
attention to detail explains why he walked through the
cabin twice, making sure no one was left behind before he
escaped the sinking plane himself.

But here's the thing: Given his personality, it is unlikely
that you would have discovered any of this without asking directly about it. When Michael Balboni, New York
State's deputy secretary for public safety, thanked him for a
job done brilliantly, he responded in the most unaffected,
humble way, "That's what we're trained to do."

Even if you had learned about all of Captain Sullenberger's activities, you might have considered his obsession dysfunctional. Wouldn't you rather hire someone well

rounded? Someone who has interests beyond the particular? Someone who might be a better communicator?

But people are often successful not despite their dysfunctions but because of them. Obsessions are one of the greatest telltale signs of success. Understand your obsessions and you will understand your natural motivation—the thing for which you would walk to the end of the earth.

Greg Davis, my friend the fishing guide, is on the water fishing with clients six days a week. Can you guess what he does on his one day off?

The fourth element is your passion, which is sometimes hard to find. One way to recover your passion is to pursue your desire. As you choose your focus for the year, pay less attention to "shoulds" and more attention to "wants."

13

Anyone Can Learn to Do a Handstand

Element Four: Pursue Your Passion (Persistence)

Many years ago, when I first started my consulting firm, a friend of mine, Elaine, who worked for a large company, suggested I speak with her colleague Colin, who might be in a position to hire Bregman Partners.

So I called Colin, mentioned Elaine, and asked to meet with him. "I'm very busy," Colin told me. "Let's just talk on the phone."

But I knew the phone wouldn't cut it. "How about lunch?" I asked him. "Or a drink after work? Or maybe just fifteen minutes in person somewhere?"

Colin finally agreed to a short lunch. Then he canceled. We rescheduled. He canceled again. We rescheduled again. He canceled again. It was clear that he didn't want to meet with me. I almost gave up.

Here's what I realized, though: If I could avoid reacting to my feelings of frustration or hurt, then the cost to me of rescheduling the meeting was a two-minute phone call with Colin's secretary. And the upside was potentially enormous.

So I kept rescheduling until, one day, several months later, Colin didn't cancel and we had lunch. It was very quick, of course, but long enough for me to ask him to let me submit a proposal. A couple of weeks after I sent it to him, he left me a short message explaining that I had missed the mark but he'd keep me in mind. Right.

I felt affronted. All that work I put in and all I got in return was a voice mail? Again, I almost walked away.

But instead, I called and asked for another lunch to understand what I misunderstood. He declined but suggested I speak with his colleague Lily, who was in a different department and might have a need for my services.

So I set up a meeting with Lily. Who canceled. As I prepared to reschedule, I noticed something unexpected: I started to enjoy the process of trying to get in, the challenge of making the sale. It became a game to me, and my goal was to keep playing until, at some point, I'd say the right thing to the right person and get my foot in the door. I was, surprisingly, having fun.

And I was getting good at it. Scheduling. Rescheduling. Finding a way to keep the conversation going. You'd think it wouldn't be something hard or useful to become good at, but you'd be wrong on both counts.

Most of our jobs hinge on repetition. That's how we become good at anything. The problem is that we give up too soon because anything we do repetitively becomes boring.

Unless, that is, we have a peculiar taste for the task; unless it captures our interest. For some reason that maybe we don't even understand—and we don't have to—we enjoy it.

That's how I learned how to do a handstand. It always seemed completely out of reach for me. But then someone told me they learned as an adult. So I figured I could learn, too. It took six months, but now I can, somewhat reliably, stand on my hands.

Which has led me to believe that anyone can do anything. As long as three conditions exist:

1. You want to achieve it.
2. You believe you can achieve it.
3. You enjoy *trying* to achieve it.

We often think we need only the first two, but it's the third condition that's most important. The trying is the day-to-day reality. And trying to achieve something is very different from achieving it. It's the opposite, actually. It's not achieving it.

If you want to be a great marketer, you need to spend years being a clumsy one. Want to be a great manager? Then you'd better enjoy being a poor one long enough to become a good one. Because that practice is what it's going to take to eventually become a great one.

In his book *Outliers*, Malcolm Gladwell discusses research

done at the Berlin Academy of Music. Researchers divided violin students into three categories: the stars, the good performers, and the ones who would become teachers but not performers. It turns out that the number one predictor of which category a violinist fell into was the number of hours of practice.

The future teachers had practiced four thousand hours in their lifetime. The good performers, eight thousand hours. And those who were categorized as stars? Every single one of them had practiced at least ten thousand hours.

And here's the compelling part: There wasn't a single violinist who had practiced ten thousand hours who wasn't a star. In other words, ten thousand hours of practice guaranteed you'd be a star violinist. According to Gladwell, ten thousand hours of practice is the magic number to become the best at anything.

Which is why you'd better enjoy *trying* to achieve your goals. Because you'll never spend ten thousand hours doing anything you don't enjoy. And if you don't enjoy the trying part, you'll never do it long enough to reach your goal.

Eventually, after five or six canceled meetings, Lily and I met for lunch. Which, as it turned out, was perfect timing. When we finally met, she had a real need, which hadn't existed when we'd first started scheduling a meeting.

By this time, I was familiar to her and the company even though I had never done any work for them. I had been around for months and they trusted me because I followed through on every commitment I made to them.

That year, I signed a large contract with Lily's company. Twelve years later, they're still a big client of Bregman Partners. And they still cancel lots of meetings.

To home in on your passion, think about what you love doing—what's important enough to you that you're willing to persist over the year, even when it feels like you're not succeeding at it.

14

A Recipe for Finding the Right Work

Element Four: Pursue Your Passion (Ease)

Do you know anyone who tried for years to have a baby but couldn't? Then, after giving up, maybe after adopting, suddenly, surprisingly, got pregnant?

Or someone who was dying to be in a relationship? Dated all the time, but never met the right person. Then, after accepting he would be alone, started focusing on other things and, lo and behold, met someone and got married?

How about someone who lost her job? Maybe she spent the next year working on her résumé, perusing job sites, devoting all her energy to getting work. All to no avail. Then, after deciding to stop looking so hard, out of the blue came a great job offer?

What is that? A karmic journey? A miracle? Statistical aberration? Pure random chance? Perhaps it never really happens; perhaps we remember those stories precisely because they are so unusual.

Or perhaps, it's a really great strategy.

I heard a story from a friend of mine. She knows a guy who's been out of work for more than a year. He's spent the year working on his résumé and sending it out. He's on Internet job sites every day. He tries to meet with people when there's the opportunity, but there aren't a lot of opportunities. And he's getting more and more depressed. It's hard to get out of bed, but he does. He puts on a suit and tie, sits at his computer, and looks. Eventually, he figures, he'll find a job. I'm sure he's right.

But probably no time soon. Who wants to hire someone who's depressed?

I do think there's another way to go through life with less pain and more success. A way to spend your year—of doing work and living your life—that's a pleasure and a great match for you and your talents.

Give up.

Not completely. But mostly. Just stop trying so hard. Here's my recipe:

1. Make a list of all the things you love doing or things that intrigue you that you'd like to try doing. This is brainstorming, so don't limit the list or judge it; write down everything you can think of.

2. Separate the activities you do with people from the activities you do alone. For example, gardening, reading, meditating, and writing are alone activities. Volunteering to run a fund-raiser is with people.

3. Look at the activities you do alone and figure out if

you can (and want to) do them in a way that includes other people. For example, join a garden club. Or a reading or meditation group. Or write something that other people read. If you can (and want to) make them activities that include other people, keep them on the list. If not, then cross them off.

4. Now's the fun part: Spend 90 percent of your time—either at work or, if you can't yet, then outside of work—doing things you love (or have always wanted to try) with other people who also love doing those things. If possible, take a leadership role.

A good friend of mine got involved in a church she adores. She loves all the pastors; she came to our house for dinner the other day and couldn't stop talking about them. So she met with them and offered to help in whatever way they needed. She's now leading a monthly strategy breakfast with the pastors and lay leaders of the church. I've never seen her so excited.

Another friend is training for a triathlon with a group of fifteen others. He's in the best shape of his life and can't stop talking about it.

A company I know is doing pro bono work for charities and the government. Everyone working on those projects is energized.

Another company I know has given all their people writing time; they've been told to put their ideas on paper and get them out there. Somewhere. Anywhere.

Why does this work? Woody Allen once said that

80 percent of success is just showing up. When I first started my business, a great mentor of mine told me to join the boards of not-for-profits and do what I do best for them. Other board members will then see the results and want to hire my company to do the same for them and their companies. That's the obvious reason.

Here's the more subtle reason this works: People want to hire energized people who are passionate and excited about what they're doing. Jobs come from being engaged in the world and building human connections.

And an even more subtle reason: If you're passionate about what you're doing, and you're doing it with other people who are passionate about what they're doing, then chances are the work you eventually end up doing for your livelihood—if you're not already doing it—will be more in line with the stuff you love to do. And then...then your life changes (not to be too dramatic, but it's true). You're doing work you love, at which you excel, with people you enjoy. You can't help but succeed.

Now, I know what you might be thinking: That's a fine strategy if you're independently wealthy, getting that nice fat trust fund check every week to pay for your gym membership (or mortgage, or kid's tuition). But what about the rest of us? We can't just quit jobs we're ill-suited for if they pay the bills. Our inability to pay the monthly bills might actually intrude on our ability to "enjoy" unemployment.

That's true. But not an excuse not to start. Because your best bet at succeeding, whether you're looking for a job or already in one, is to throw yourself into things you adore.

Work that doesn't feel like work because it's *easy*. Because you naturally shine when you're doing it.

If you don't have a job, then your hardest job is to manage your fear. Because here's the kicker: It won't take longer to find a job even though you're spending less time looking. It'll take you less time.

Pursuing things you love doing with people you enjoy will better position you to get a job—and much better position you to get a job at the intersection of the four elements. Other people will notice your commitment, passion, skill, and personality, and they'll want to either hire you or help you get hired.

Also, actively pursuing other activities while looking for a job will make you more qualified for a job—because you'll end up a more interesting person. When you finally get that job interview, you'll be able to recount all the many things you've been doing (and will probably have a good time relating them) instead of saying that the only thing you've been doing for the past three years is looking (unsuccessfully so far) for a job.

I just heard the story of a woman who decided to do work she didn't enjoy for a few years in order to make a lot of money. Three years later, the company went bankrupt. That could happen to anyone. Bad luck. But here's what she said that I found the most depressing: "It's as though I didn't work for the last three years—it's all gone. And what's worse, I worked like a dog and hated it. I just wasted three years of my life."

Don't waste your time, your year. Spend it in a way

that excites you. That teaches you new things. That introduces you to new people who see you at your natural, most excited, most powerful best. Use and develop your strengths. Use and even develop your weaknesses. Express your differences. And pursue the things you love.

There's no better way to spend your year.

Your year will be best spent doing work that you enjoy so much, it feels effortless. You'll always work tirelessly at your passions—hard work will feel easier.

15

What Matters to You?

Element Four: Pursue Your Passion (Meaning)

I was lying in bed, reading a magazine, when the fear arose. It started somewhere between my stomach and my chest, and it radiated outward. Like adrenaline coursing through my body after a sudden fright, it was a physical sensation, but it felt slower, deeper, wider, as it radiated to the tops of my arms and legs. It felt hot. I started to sweat. My body felt weak.

I put down the magazine and lay with my head on the pillow as I thought about death.

My mother-in-law was diagnosed with cancer; she died after a decades-long battle with the disease. A few months after her death, I received a call from a friend of mine, in her forties, who one morning found a lump in her breast and a few days later had a mastectomy. A few days after that, a friend told me his business partner came home from vacation feeling a little under the weather; within a week he was dead from an aggressive cancer he never knew he had. That was right after he told me that his father-in-law was recently killed crossing the street.

And here I was now, reading an article by Atul Gawande about rethinking end-of-life medical treatment. Gawande isn't just insightful as he explores what doctors should do when they can't save your life, he's also vivid. The first line of his article reads: "Sara Thomas Monopoli was pregnant with her first child when her doctors learned that she was going to die."

I am, as far as I know, thank God, healthy. But it was somewhere in the middle of that article that it suddenly hit me—not just intellectually, but physically and emotionally: *I am going to die.*

Each year, the U.S. Bureau of Labor Statistics conducts an American Time Use Survey, asking thousands of Americans to document how they spend every minute of every day.

According to the data, most of us spend a total of almost 20 hours of each day sleeping (8.68 hours/day), working (7.78 hours/day), and watching television (3.45 hours/day). I know: Shocking, right? I mean, who sleeps that much?

It's hard to look at the data and not think about where you fit in. Do you watch more or less television? Do you work longer or shorter hours? It's a useful and interesting exercise to examine how we spend each minute of the day. To know where we're devoting our wisdom, our action, our life's energy.

And yet *where* we spend our time tells us only so much.

More important, and completely subjective, is what those activities *mean* to us.

I recently happened upon a short article, "Top Five Regrets of the Dying" by Bronnie Ware, who spent many years nursing people who had gone home to die. Their most common regret? "I wish I'd had the courage to live a life true to myself, not the life others expected of me." Their second most common? "I wish I didn't work so hard."

There are two ways to address these regrets. One, work less hard and spend your time living a life true to yourself. Or two, work just as hard—harder even—on things that matter to you. On things that represent a life lived true to you. Something you consider to be important. Meaningful.

Because if you put those two regrets together, you realize that what people really regret isn't simply working so hard, it's working so hard on things that simply don't matter to them. If our work feels like it matters to us, if it represents *a life true to us*, then we would die without the main regrets that haunt the dying. We would live more fully.

That doesn't mean you should sell all your belongings and feed the poor in a foreign country. Well, if that's true to you, go ahead. But the whole point is that your life needs to be true to *you*, not what others expect of you. Maybe that's feeding the poor. Maybe it's cooking dinner for your family.

So the question is: *What matters to you?*

That's a critically important question to explore. What matters to you? Of course making enough money, having enough vacation time, and feeling loved and respected by your family and friends matter. But you know that already. Go deeper.

First, ask yourself what's working: What about your daily work, your daily life, matters to you? Why are you doing it? What part of your life is a source of pride? What impact do you feel you're having on people, ideas, or things that are important to you?

Next, ask yourself what's neutral: What are you spending your time on that you don't particularly care about? What doesn't matter to you? What's not important?

Finally, ask yourself what alienates you: What are you spending your time on—in work or in life—that contradicts what matters to you? What makes you feel bad? Untrue to yourself? What are you, even slightly, embarrassed about?

And then slowly, over time, shift where you're spending that time, so the scale begins to tip in the direction of what matters to you. Some things you won't be able to change immediately: Maybe you're working in the wrong job, for the wrong company. But don't be afraid to ask the questions; you will be tremendously more dedicated, productive, and effective if you care. If you're working on things that matter to you.

Can everyone spend their time working on things that matter to them? Maybe not. But I remember listening to a nighttime janitor as she spoke with such deep pride about how well she cleaned, how wonderful the office looked after she finished, and how important she felt it was to the people who worked there during the day. So, maybe yes.

There is no objective measure—certainly not money—that determines the value of a particular kind of work to the person who does it. All that matters is that you do work that matters to you.

I woke up at six in the morning and looked over at my bedside table where Gawande's article lay open, the photo of an empty wheelchair with a baby's HAPPY BIRTHDAY balloon tied to it staring at me. Once again, I felt that dreaded rush of fear and sadness spread from the center of my chest to the rest of my body.

So I took a deep breath, got out of bed, took a shower, and sat down to write this chapter. To work on this book. Because writing, to me, matters.

Focus your year on the things that matter to you. On things that have specific meaning to you.

16

I'm the Parent I Have to Be

Avoiding Tunnel Vision

Wait a minute, I thought as I looked up from the trail we had been hiking for several hours. *Where are we?*

I knew I was lost. Unfortunately, I wasn't alone. I was leading a thirty-day wilderness expedition for the National Outdoor Leadership School (NOLS). Which, in this case, meant there were eight 16- to 24-year-old students following me.

For most of an expedition, NOLS groups travel off trail. We use topographic maps that reflect the physical features of an area—mountains, streams, valleys, ridges—and we navigate through the wilderness by comparing what we see around us with what's on the map.

Each morning we agree on our goal—where we plan to camp at the end of the day—and then choose a rough path through the wilderness. We know the general direction we're moving and maintain our course by paying attention to the environment—keep that mountain to the left, that small river to the right, and that craggy peak in front.

Every once in a while there happens to be a trail that travels in the same direction we're traveling so we follow it. It makes for easy walking.

But a dangerous thing happens when we follow a trail: We stop paying attention to the environment. Since the trail is so easy to follow, we allow our minds to wander and neglect to observe where we are.

Then we forge ahead, moving with speed and purpose, right to the point where we look up and realize, as I did that day, that the environment around us is no longer recognizable. Our focus blinded us.

This is not just a hiking thing.

In business and in life, we set all kinds of goals—build a company, meet sales objectives, be a supportive manager— and then we define a strategy for achieving each of them. The goal is the destination; the strategy is our trail to get there.

Only sometimes we get so absorbed in the trail—in how we're going to achieve the goal, in our method or process—that we lose sight of the destination, of where we were going in the first place. We walk right by the opportunities that would have propelled us forward toward our planned destination.

Which is what happened to Sammy, a religious man who was caught in his house during a flood. He climbed up to his roof and prayed, asking God to save him.

Sammy saw a wood plank in the water and let it float

by. "God will rescue me," he said to himself. After some time, a man came by in a boat and offered him a lift, but Sammy declined. "God will rescue me," he told the man. The water continued to rise; it was up to his neck when a helicopter flew overhead. Sammy waved it off, saying, "God will rescue me." Finally, Sammy drowned.

Next thing he knew, Sammy was in heaven, where he was greeted by God. "Why didn't you rescue me?" Sammy asked.

"I tried!" God answered. "I sent a wood plank, I sent a boat, I sent a helicopter..."

Okay, so it's not a true story, but the point is still useful. Sammy was so committed to his strategy of God saving him that he missed the rescue.

I started my company more than twelve years ago with a fifty-page business plan. It was a very useful tool—it kept me focused, helped me avoid mistakes, enabled me to settle on a growth strategy. But if you look at my company today, it looks nothing like that plan.

Because the economy changed, I changed, my clients changed, and the opportunities changed. If I had stuck to my plan, I would have failed. It was keeping my eye on the changing environment, and being willing to toss the plan and create a new one in sync with new realities, that enabled me to grow my business.

I remember hearing a mother speak about how difficult it was for her to parent her autistic child. "I'm not the parent I planned to be," she said. "I'm the parent I have to be."

I've noticed the same thing about great managers. They might have a plan for how they want to manage. But they're constantly shifting that plan based on the strengths and weaknesses of the people they're managing.

Monitor and adjust. That's the key to effective leadership, indoors or out.

On the trail, I stopped my group of students and admitted that I had gotten us lost. I explained how being too focused on the trail can easily lead us astray.

"Great," answered a sixteen-year-old boy sarcastically. "So how do we get unlost?"

"You tell me."

"Look at the map?" he suggested.

"And your surroundings!" I added.

Pausing every once in a while to look at your surroundings—to reconnect with your personal guideposts, your strengths, weaknesses, differences, and passions—can prevent you from being lulled into unconscious movement in the wrong direction.

Staying connected to your guideposts will help you avoid tunnel vision and keep you moving in the right direction.

17

I've Missed More Than Nine Thousand Shots

Avoiding Surrender After Failure

Peter, I'd like you to stay for a minute after class," said Calvin, who teaches my favorite body conditioning class at the gym.

"What'd I do?" I asked him.

"It's what you didn't do."

"What didn't I do?"

"Fail."

"You kept me after class for *not* failing?"

"This"—he began to mimic my casual weight-lifting style, using weights that were obviously too light—"is not going to get you anywhere. A muscle only grows if you work it until it fails. You need to use more challenging weights. You need to fail."

Calvin's on to something.

Every time I ask a room of executives to list the top five moments their career took a leap forward—not just a step, but a leap—failure is always on the list. For some it was the loss of a job. For others it was a project gone bad. And for others still it was the failure of a larger system, like an economic downturn, that required them to step up.

Yet most of us spend tremendous effort trying to avoid even the possibility of failure. According to Dr. Carol Dweck, professor at Stanford University, we have a mind-set problem. Dweck has done an enormous amount of research to understand what makes someone give up in the face of adversity versus strive to overcome it.

It turns out the answer is deceptively simple: It's all in your head.

If you believe that your talents are inborn or fixed, then you will try to avoid failure at all costs because failure is proof of your limitation. People with a fixed mind-set like to solve the same problems over and over again. It reinforces their sense of competence.

Children with fixed mind-sets would rather redo an easy jigsaw puzzle than try a harder one. Students with fixed mind-sets would rather not learn new languages. CEOs with fixed mind-sets will surround themselves with people who agree with them. They feel smart when they get it right.

But if you believe your talent grows with persistence and effort, then you seek failure as an opportunity to improve. People with a growth mind-set feel smart when they're learning, not when they're flawless.

Michael Jordan, arguably the world's best basketball player, has a growth mind-set. Most successful people do. In high school, he was cut from the basketball team. But obviously that didn't discourage him: "I've missed more than 9,000 shots in my career. I've lost almost 300 games. Twenty-six times I've been trusted to take the game-winning shot and missed. I've failed over and over and over again in my life. And that is why I succeed."

If you have a growth mind-set, then you use your failures to improve. If you have a fixed mind-set, you may never fail, but neither do you learn or grow.

In business, we have to be discriminating about when we choose to challenge ourselves. In high-risk, high-leverage situations, it's better to stay within your current capability. In lower-risk situations, where the consequences of failure are less significant, better to push the envelope. The important point is to know that pushing the envelope, that failing, is how you learn and grow and succeed. It's your opportunity.

Here's the good news: You can change your success by changing your mind-set. When Dweck trained children to view themselves as capable of growing their intelligence, they worked harder, more persistently, and with greater success on math problems they had previously abandoned as unsolvable.

A growth mind-set is the secret to maximizing potential. Want to grow your staff? Give them tasks above their abilities. They don't think they can do it? Tell them you expect them to work at it for a while, struggle with it. That it will take more time than the tasks they're used to doing. That you expect they'll make some mistakes along the way. But you know they can do it.

Want to increase your own performance? Set high goals where you have a 50 to 70 percent chance of success. According to the late David McClelland, psychologist and Harvard researcher, that's the sweet spot for high achievers. Then, when you fail half the time, figure out what you should do differently and try again. That's practice. And, as we saw earlier, ten thousand hours of that kind of practice will make you an expert in anything. No matter where you start.

The next class I did with Calvin, I doubled the weight I was using. Yeah, that's right. Unfortunately, that gave me tendonitis in my elbow, which I'm nursing with rest and ice. Sometimes you can fail even when you're trying to fail.

Hey, I'm learning.

Failure is inevitable, useful, and educational. Just don't give up—stay focused over the year—and it will pay off.

18

When the Future Is Uncertain

Avoiding Paralysis

There is something curious about a group of houses in Utah. They're falling apart. Windows covered with wood. Roofs patched with blue tarp, blowing in the wind. Walls simply missing.

And yet people live in them. These houses are not being built; they are half built. This has nothing to do with the real estate crash. It's not a consequence of poverty, nor is it a design statement.

The houses' inhabitants simply aren't motivated to finish them. You see, they're fundamentalist Mormons who have been excommunicated by the mainstream Mormon church for their practice of polygamy. And their last known leader, Warren Jeffs, had a penchant for predicting the end of the world on a rolling six-months basis.

If you think the world is about to end, what's the point of fixing your house?

When I described these houses to Anne, a senior

leader of a large retail bank, her face contorted with recognition.

"That's exactly what I'm doing!" she said.

"Living in an unfinished house?" I asked.

"Yes!" She told me she hadn't done her usual quarterly all-hands call with her team.

"Why not?" I asked.

"What's there to say?" Anne responded. "Nothing's clear. I have no idea what to tell them. Will they be in their roles in two months? Will their priorities change? Will we even exist? There's too much uncertainty."

She knew it was a mistake not to do the all-hands call. And yet, she admitted to me, she hadn't done many of her normal management routines. She regularly canceled meetings with her direct reports and even skipped their performance reviews and career development conversations.

Why have a career development conversation with someone when there's a good chance they may not have a career with you at all? You're super-busy, understaffed, stressed, and feeling vulnerable yourself.

On top of all that, the people who report to you aren't pushing for conversations, either. Sure, they want some answers. But they're lying low. Keeping their heads down, trying not to make a splash. Because if you happen to be working on that layoff plan when they come by, you might take notice and add their name to the list. So they try to look busy. And they take the long way to the bathroom to avoid your office.

Here's the problem: When our future is uncertain, we have a hard time functioning in the present.

So what should you do?

David McClelland, the Harvard psychology professor introduced a little earlier, wrote the book *Human Motivation*. It's 688 pages long, but since the world might end in six months, I'll give you the short version. Everyone is driven by three things:

1. Achievement (the desire to compete against increasingly challenging goals)
2. Affiliation (the desire to be liked/loved)
3. Power, expressed in one of two ways:
   ◦ Personalized (the desire for influence and respect for yourself)
   ◦ Socialized (the desire to empower others; to offer them influence and respect)

If people have the opportunity to achieve, affiliate, and influence, they'll be motivated and engaged. Even without a clear vision of the future.

So instead of worrying about what life is going to be like tomorrow, focus on these three things today.

Answer these three questions:

1. Are you working on something meaningful and challenging—something for which you have about a 50 percent chance of succeeding?

2. Are you relating to other people at work or socially—
    people you like and to whom you feel close?
3. Do you feel recognized for the work you are doing—
    paid or unpaid? Can you influence decisions and out-
    comes?

If the answer is yes in each case, great. You'll be motivated. Wherever it's not, create those opportunities immediately.

Make sure you have clear goals and the autonomy to
achieve them. Make sure you are working on something
you find challenging and interesting.

And find opportunities to collaborate (and celebrate)
with others. This is especially important because at times
of uncertainty, people become more political. They start to
suspect that their colleagues are trying to be noticed, take
more credit, work on better projects. But as they work on
projects collaboratively, their trust grows.

Also, look for opportunities to offer input on how things
should be done. And if necessary, ask that your participa-
tion be recognized.

Anne realized that even though she was a "leader" in
the bank, she too was paralyzed by the uncertainty of the
future.

A few weeks after speaking with Anne, I met with her
again and she told me she had held one-on-one meetings
with each of her managers that week. In those meetings,
she made sure each person had some kind of challenging, meaningful project to work on. She also made sure

each had at least one project that involved collaboration with other people. She told me that the third motivator was harder because it felt fake to recognize people for something they had done when she didn't feel they had been doing much. She did give them influence over how they were going to achieve their projects, and as they made headway, she was looking for opportunities to recognize them.

Doing this had a side benefit for Anne. She was considerably more energized when I last saw her. Following through on this plan tapped into her motivation. It was challenging (achievement), helped her connect to the people with whom she worked (affiliation) and enabled her to enable others (power).

But Anne took it a step further. She also went to her own manager and had the same conversation with him. She went over her projects, and together they set goals she felt—but was not certain—she could achieve. Goals she felt played to her strengths, allowed for her weaknesses, used her unique talents, and about which she felt passionate.

Then she asked that two other people—colleagues whom she enjoyed—be allowed to collaborate on the projects with her. And she set a date with her manager when he would review the work and, if appropriate, publicly recognize her for the work she and her colleagues had done.

Sound contrived? Maybe. But it still works. And sometimes it takes some contriving to get what you want.

Especially if the future is uncertain, your goals are not

clear, and you feel paralyzed in terms of moving forward. Perhaps you don't know exactly what this next year should be about. Perhaps you're not crystal clear about your goals for the year or what you want to achieve.

That's okay. As long as you create the right environment—one in which you feel challenged, loved, and respected—then you'll be motivated enough to keep moving in the right direction. Even without a plan. Even without a destination.

So it's time to choose. Do you want to live in a half-built house while you wait for the end of the world? As it turns out, some people have been living in those houses for *years*.

Or do you want to be like Anne and spend whatever time you have fixing your house, along with your colleagues?

The world may end in six months, but at least those six months can be filled with engaging work, connected community, and empowered action.

> *Don't be paralyzed by an uncertain future. Just keep moving.*

19

Maybe

Avoiding the Rush to Judgment

There is a Buddhist story about a poor farmer whose one horse ran away. All his neighbors came to him in sympathy, saying, "What bad luck!"

"Maybe," he responded.

The next day, the horse returned with several other wild horses. "What great luck!" his neighbors exclaimed.

"Maybe," he responded.

A few days later, the farmer's son was trying to tame one of the wild horses when he was thrown off and broke his leg. "What terrible luck!" his neighbors said.

"Maybe," he responded.

A week later, the army came through the village to draft all the young men, but—seeing the broken leg of the farmer's son—they left him in peace. "What wonderful luck!" the neighbors said.

"Maybe," the farmer responded. And so it goes.

My life has been a series of lucky accidents strung

together starting from the moment of my conception, which occurred despite my parents' best birth control efforts.

In college, I was planning to go into politics. Then, in the spring of my junior year, the bicycle trip I had planned to go on was canceled because the leader broke her arm. So instead, I went on a camping trip, and it changed my life. I gave up politics and began teaching leadership on wilderness expeditions. On one of those expeditions, I met Eleanor, who would eventually become my wife.

Later, I built a successful company teaching leadership with lots of employees and several offices around the world. Then, as luck would have it, my company crashed along with the economy and the Twin Towers. It turns out, after some introspection and a solid dose of therapy, that I wasn't enjoying the business the way I had built it the first time. So I rebuilt it in a much smaller, more sustainable, more fulfilling way.

While I might not have been happy about it at the time, each turn of luck was a catalyst that brought me closer to the life I'm happily living now.

Often, we operate with the impression that we are in control of our lives. I remember long conversations with Eleanor about exactly when we should have our second child. Two miscarriages later, we realized it wasn't up to us. And when Sophia eventually came, we knew that anytime would have been the right time.

Some strokes of luck are small. Maybe you enjoy a conversation with someone new. Maybe you read a poem that happens to be sitting on someone's desk. Maybe you bump into the car in front of you. Only years later can you see how fundamentally that moment may have changed your life.

Some strokes of luck are big, and you know at the time they will change your life. Maybe you win $10 million with a lottery ticket you didn't even know you had, as happened to a woman in Australia. Maybe you lose your job.

What we don't know is how those things will change our lives. All the research points to how poor we are at predicting how we'll feel about something once it happens to us. Lottery winners are no happier than before. Paraplegics are no less happy.

And there's something I've been noticing about some people who have lost their jobs. They seem happier. Relieved, almost. Not everyone. But in many cases, the fear of losing your job is worse than losing your job. I know a large number of employed people who are miserable on two counts: They hate their jobs, and they're afraid of losing them. They're scared and stuck.

But once you lose your job, you can move on. Daniel Gilbert, professor of psychology at Harvard University, explained this phenomenon in a *New York Times* article: "When we get bad news we weep for a while, and then get busy making the best of it. We change our behavior, we change our attitudes...[but] an uncertain future leaves us stranded in an unhappy present with nothing to do but wait."

So when your luck changes, what should you do about it?

Remember Stanford psychologist Carol Dweck, whom we met a few chapters ago? She's done an enormous amount of research to understand what makes someone give up in the face of adversity rather than strive to overcome it. Her research shows that if someone believes his talent is inborn he'll give up quickly, because any obstacle is a sign of his limitation. He's hit a wall; he can't do something and won't ever be able to.

But if someone believes his talent grows with persistence and effort, he'll work to master the challenge. He'll view adversity as an opportunity to get better.

So here's the good news: You can change your results by changing your mind-set. Remember, when Dweck trained children to view themselves as capable of growing their intelligence, they worked harder, more persistently, and with greater success on math problems they had previously abandoned as unsolvable.

Luck changes. Call it fate. Call it God's will. Call it an accident. No matter how well we plan our lives, we're not fully in control. But how we face our luck—good and bad—is in our control.

How's this year going so far? Are you having good luck? Bad luck?

Maybe.

But if you leverage your strengths, embrace your weaknesses, assert your differences, and pursue your passions, you can be confident that you are spending your time in the right places, doing the right things, no matter the short-term result. That thinking will keep you grounded through your successes and your failures.

> *The time to judge your successes or failures is never.*

20

What Is This Year About?

Creating Your Annual Focus

It's a buffet?" I asked my wife Eleanor, about a Sunday brunch we were going to with her parents.

"Yes," she answered, a worried look on her face. "You gonna be okay?"

"Sure," I said smiling. "I love buffets."

"I know," she said, looking even more worried.

Sure enough, a few hours later, I was completely stuffed. Couldn't possibly have fit another thing in me. And yet, somehow, I managed to go back for a little more dessert.

Here's my problem with buffets: so many choices. And all for one price. It's a killer combination.

I happen to love variety and the opportunity to taste all the different dishes. So I get a little of everything. But a little of everything adds up to a lot. And I leave the buffet uncomfortable, exhausted, and regretting it.

Yet somehow, even though I know better, I do it every time.

This buffet challenge is the same challenge we face when managing our time. Because there's so much to do—so many interesting people, enjoyable activities, worthwhile causes, compelling opportunities—it's hard to choose. So we don't. We try to do it all.

The problem with most time management systems is that they don't help solve the problem: They're focused on how to get it all done in less time. But that's a mistake. Just like tasting from a buffet is a mistake. Because we can't possibly get it all done and not end up frantic, depleted, and overwhelmed.

The secret to surviving a buffet is to eat fewer things. And the secret to thriving in your life is the same: Do fewer things.

Which means you have to be strategic about what you choose to do, and make hard decisions about what you choose not to do.

So let's get concrete here. How many things should we focus on? After a tremendous amount of trial and error—mostly error—I've come to the number five.

I've decided to focus my year on five things. Three work-related, two personal. (Almost) everything I do must fit in one of these five areas. If it doesn't, then I politely decline.

Why five? Because for me, it seems to work. It covers the most important things that need to get done, and it's not overwhelming. It's enough. On the other hand, you may come up with three. Or seven. And if that works for you, then go with it. You'll know if it works for you because you'll feel accomplished in each of the categories without getting confused, feeling overwhelmed, or dropping balls.

Why a year? Because a lifetime is too much and a month is too little. A year is the right-size chunk for our long-term focus. We think in terms of years—schools, birthdays, religious and secular holiday cycles, salaries, bonuses, and performance reviews all operate within the framework of a year—and a year provides us with the perfect amount of time in which to make real progress in our lives without getting lost.

So what should your five (or so) things be? That depends on your life. Here are mine:

Business

1. Do Great Work with Current Clients
2. Attract Future Clients
3. Write and Speak About My Ideas

Personal

1. Be Present with Family and Friends
2. Have Fun and Take Care of Myself

Most of these are not clearly measurable. That's okay. They're not goals. Not everything has to be a goal. They're areas of focus. They're where you want to spend your time. If you want, you could create specific goals in each category.

Your list will be different because you're different. What's important is that you intentionally create the list. What are the five things you want to focus on over the next year? They should be substantial things, so when you spend your time on them, you'll get to the end of the year and know it was time well spent.

In other words, step up to the buffet with a plate that has enough room for five different foods and no more. Since you're selecting only five, make sure they are nourishing and tasty.

What's the time equivalent of nourishing and tasty? Make sure that your list leverages your strengths, embraces your weaknesses, asserts your differences, and reflects your passions. It's also important that it includes opportunities to be challenged, opportunities to work with others, and opportunities to be recognized.

Once you've made sure your five (or so) areas of focus reflect those elements, then make tough decisions about what doesn't fit on your plate.

I decided to step down from the board of an organization, though I found it very worthwhile, because it took a considerable amount of time and didn't clearly fit in my five. Still, contributing to the community is important to me. So now I do service work with my family. It's part of the category *Be Present with Family and Friends*.

When you decide on your five, commit to spending 95 percent of your time there. The other 5 percent is miscellaneous. Maybe a project on your colleague Jane's top five doesn't make your top five, but she needs your help. Maybe you need to take the car in for an oil change. Maybe you *need* to read all the reviews about the iPad (and then wait in line to buy one). Those are all fine uses of your 5 percent. But if it becomes 20 percent, it means you're spending too much time on other people's priorities, your frivolity, and life maintenance, and not enough time on your own priorities.

Sometimes you'll be faced with conflicts between your categories. I faced that conflict when I was asked to speak at a TEDx conference in Mexico. I think TED and TEDx conferences are fantastic. And my speaking there clearly fit into my priority of *Write and Speak About My Ideas.* But the date conflicted with a party celebrating Eleanor's fortieth birthday and her father's seventieth. It was tempting, and I'd be lying if I said I didn't consider it. But ultimately I declined the conference.

There's no formula for deciding how to prioritize within the five. But when a conflict arises, think about it, and most of the time you'll know what to do. If you don't, here's a way to decide: Think about where you've been spending most of your time lately. If one of the five has been getting the short end of the stick, then choose in favor of that one to balance it out.

And if you still can't decide? Then pick either—at least you'll know they're both worthwhile choices because they're both in your five.

Last week was the first time in many months that I went to a buffet. I walked up to the line with a little trepidation and a lot of resolve. I felt a little sad, a little conflicted, as

I passed up so many good-looking dishes. It wasn't easy. It took self-control. But I stuck to one plate, five different choices.

And for the first time I left a buffet feeling good.

Focus your year on the five areas that will make the most difference in your life.

Where We Are

Leverage your strengths, embrace your weaknesses, assert your differences, and pursue your passions. That's the recipe for the tastiest and most nourishing year. And for a life that will satisfy and reward you. By avoiding a few pitfalls—fear of failure, paralysis, tunnel vision, the rush to judgment—you can keep eating well all year long.

But even after you've established your annual focus—the areas where you should be spending most of your time—life gets busy. Days get filled with all sorts of obligations—some important and some not— that will entice you away from the things you decided and know are important.

The solution is in a day. Because a year is lived one day at a time. So how should you spend those days? That's the focus of part 3.

PART THREE

What Is This Day About?

Get the Right Things Done

It's one thing—one *huge* thing—to decide where you want to focus your year. Most people never really think about it as they work furiously toward...well, they're not really sure.

Still, it's another thing entirely to *actually spend* your time focusing—day in and day out—on where you've decided to focus.

This challenge took me a little by surprise.

I had pressed that FIND ME button and flown up in the air, hovering over my life with a bird's-eye view. I had explored different sides of me—actor, doctor, rabbi, investment manager—and had come to the revelation that I could integrate all these sides while remaining a consultant. In fact, integrating them would make me a *better, more valuable* consultant. I just had to change *how* I was consulting so that I could fully express my strengths, weaknesses, differences, and passions.

And I descended back to earth in a slightly different location, one more suited to who I was, who I chose to be. A location from which I could make better—more focused, deliberate, profitable, and meaningful—use of my time. I was thrilled, having found a home that fit, having articulated areas of focus that I would enjoy and at which I would excel.

Then came Monday morning.

Somehow, even though I had tremendous clarity, I still kept doing everything I was doing beforehand. I kept selling the same projects. I kept calling other consultants to do the work with, and for, me. I kept repeating the patterns that would keep me right where I was, instead of move me to where I planned on going.

I tried to change direction. I thought about it. One week, I spent a few hours trying to write an article. But it didn't go anywhere and I got involved in other work, work I considered at the time to be "real" work, and I gave up.

A few months later, when I was no further along in my plan, I realized that I needed a system. Something that would help me be disciplined and methodical about where I spent my time.

I looked at all sorts of time management systems but they were either too complicated, too time consuming to implement, or too focused on getting everything done.

But that was already my problem: I was trying to get everything done and, in the end, the only things I got done were the things that screamed the loudest.

Over time, I developed my own system to keep myself

centered on my areas of focus and to help me ignore the things that were distracting me. So that with each step I took—each action I chose, each call I made, each time I sat at my computer—I moved further in the direction I had set out for my career and my life.

A daily plan helped me tremendously. I structured my day so it supported me in becoming the kind of consultant I wanted to become. That meant making explicit decisions, ahead of time, about where I would spend my time and where I wouldn't. It meant lists and to-dos—but not too many—and a calendar that truly reflected who I was and what I was trying to accomplish. And it meant gentle, but consistent, reminders to stay on track.

Because doing work that matters is much harder than doing work that doesn't. And the desire to escape from hard, meaningful work is ever-present. So it helps to have some structure—not so much that it gets in the way, but enough so you keep moving forward deliberately and intentionally.

Each morning, I ask myself some questions: Am I prepared for this day? Prepared to make it a successful, productive day? Have I thought about it? Planned for it? Anticipated the risks that might take me off track? Will my plan for this day keep me focused on what my year is about?

The chapters in this section will guide you to prepare for—and live—each day so you can answer those questions with a resounding "Yes!" After considering the importance of looking ahead, we'll explore the best way to create a plan for what *to* do based on your annual focus, while consciously choosing what *not* to do so you don't get distracted. We'll look at how to use your calendar to ensure you actually get all your to-dos done. And we'll see how a short beep and a few minutes in the evening can help you stay on track. Finally, we'll pull it all together in the 18-minute plan itself, your key to getting the right things done each day.

This section will pave your path to a fulfilling day that brings you one strong step closer to a fulfilling year.

21

Dude, What Happened?

Planning Ahead

Win, my mountain biking partner, and I looked down the ten-foot drop.

"Should be fun," he said as we backed away from the edge and climbed up the hill to get some runway. I wasn't so sure. He got on his bike, pedaled to get a little speed, and took the plunge, effortlessly gliding over the rocks, roots, and stumps.

My turn. I felt the adrenaline rush as I clipped my feet into the pedals. My heart was beating fast. My hands were shaking. I took a few tentative pedal strokes forward and inched up. I felt my front tire go over the edge and I started to descend, checking my speed as I weaved around the obstacles.

Suddenly I hit something, and my bike abruptly stopped. Unfortunately, I didn't. I flew over my handlebars and ended up on the ground, lying beside my bike, front wheel still spinning.

"Dude," Win said, laughing, "you okay?"

"Yeah." I brushed the dirt off my elbows. "Dude, what happened?"

Neither of us knew. So I picked up my bike, climbed the chute, and did it again. Not just the chute, the whole thing: the adrenaline, the weaving around the obstacles, the abrupt stop, the flying over the handlebars.

"Dude," Win laughed again. I was officially in the movie *Groundhog Day*. I climbed back up the chute and did it again. And again. I must have done it five times before I figured out what was stopping me.

Me.

A mountain bike has to be moving fast enough to make it over an obstacle. The bigger the obstacle, the more momentum the bike wheel needs to roll over it. There was one big unavoidable rock, and each time I came upon it I unconsciously squeezed on my brake. That slowed me down just enough to turn the rock into an insurmountable wall.

I needed more speed to keep moving, so I climbed back up and did it again. I stared at the rock and picked up speed, keeping my eyes on it right to the point where I squeezed on my brakes and flipped over my handlebars again.

I knew what I had to do, but I couldn't do it. It was just too scary. As long as I was focused on the rock, I couldn't prevent myself from braking.

But I wasn't ready to give up. So I climbed back up and tried one more time. This time, I decided to focus ahead of me—ten feet in front of where I was at any point in time. So I would see the rock when it was ten feet away, but I wouldn't be looking at it when I was going over it.

It worked. I slid easily over the rock and made it down the chute without falling.

I'm a huge proponent of living in the present. If you pay attention to what's happening now, the future will take care of itself. You know: Don't regret the past; don't worry about the future; just be here now and all that.

But sometimes, focusing on the present is the obstacle. Take driving a car, for example. If you didn't look ahead to see where the road was going, you'd keep driving straight and crash at the next curve. When you're driving, you never actually pay attention to where you are; you're always paying attention to what's happening in the road ahead, and you change course based on what you see in the future.

It's the same with your day. Some days, I remind myself of me mountain biking down that chute. Doing whatever appears in front of me, when it appears in front of me. I don't think about a meeting until I'm in the meeting. I don't think about what's most important to get done until, well, until it doesn't get done. When someone appears in front of me and asks for something, that's who I end up attending to. Even if it's not the right priority.

Effectively navigating a day is the same as effectively navigating down a rocky precipice on a mountain bike. We need to look ahead. Plan the route. And then follow through.

"You done?" Win asked me, waiting not so patiently at the bottom of the chute.

"Yeah, I think I figured it out."

"Let's go then." And with that, he was off in a blaze down the trail.

Plan your day ahead so you can fly through it, successfully maneuvering and moving toward your intended destination.

22

Bird by Bird

Deciding What to Do

So how's it going?" I asked Fiorella, the head of sales at a midsize technology company that's a client of mine. Fiorella and I speak once a week.

"I have a tremendous amount on my plate," she responded. "I have performance issues with several salespeople in Asia; my U.S. team doesn't seem to get the new direction we're moving in—or if they do get it, they're resisting it. Also, I need to have a strategy conversation with Jean [the head of Europe] and a different one with Leena [the CEO], and that's just the first few things on my to-do list."

She needed a minute to take a breath. What she said next surprised me.

"There's so much to do," she said, "that it's hard to get anything done."

Her statement surprised me, but it shouldn't have, because I've experienced the same thing. You'd think it would be the opposite—that when we have a lot to do, we become very productive in order to get it done—and sometimes that happens.

But often, especially when we have *too* much to do, we freeze. Or we move frantically, spinning without traction.

Because when there's so much competing for attention, we don't know where to begin, so we don't begin anywhere.

It reminds me of a research study conducted by Dr. Sheena Iyengar, the management professor at Columbia University Business School, whom I wrote about several chapters ago. As you might recall, this was the study where a group of people was offered samples of six different jams available for purchase while another group was presented with twenty-four different jams. The six-jam group was ten times more likely to actually purchase a jam. Because the greater the options, the more difficult it becomes to choose a single one, so we end up choosing none.

That's what happens when we've got too many things to do. We look busy. We seem to be moving. But in reality, we get very little done.

In those moments, we need a way to disperse the fog of overwhelm. We need to break down the tasks into chunks and begin to work through them.

Anne Lamott describes this moment beautifully in her book *Bird By Bird: Some Instructions on Writing and Life.* "Thirty years ago my older brother, who was ten years old at the time, was trying to get a report on birds written that he'd had three months to write. It was due the next day.

We were out at our family cabin in Bolinas, and he was at the kitchen table close to tears, surrounded by binder paper and pencils and unopened books on birds, immobilized by the hugeness of the task ahead. Then my father sat down beside him, put his arm around my brother's shoulder, and said, 'Bird by bird, buddy. Just take it bird by bird.'"

That's great advice. It's like paying down credit card debt. You may have a huge, intimidating amount to pay. But there's only one way to responsibly handle it: week by week. Each week, put a little aside—more than the interest and more than you're adding to the card—and eventually it will get paid off.

But our lives are more scattered and complex than a report on birds or credit card debt. So we need another level of organization, not to make sure that *everything* gets done but to make sure the *right* things get done.

That's where a structured to-do list can be helpful. But it has to be simple—otherwise, creating your to-do list becomes one more thing on your to-do list. Thankfully, you've already got the structure.

You already know the five (or so) things your year is about. Well, those things need to be the foundation—the organizing map—for your day. Because, like paying down credit card debt, the way to make an impact on your areas of focus for the year is by spending your time focusing on those areas. Every day.

So when you create your to-do list, do it in the categories of your five things. Then add a sixth category, titled *The Other 5%*. Mine, for a particular day, looks like this:

Do Great Work with Current Clients	Attract Future Clients
○ Call John to set up interviews. ○ Create feedback report for Lily. ○ Design strategy offsite for X, Inc. ○ Set up travel for Portland trip. ○ Create plan for coaching session with Larry.	○ Call Paul re: retainer.
Write and Speak About My Ideas	**Be Present with Family and Friends**
○ Write blog post for this week. ○ Write book chapter on to-do list. ○ Set up meeting with speaking agent. ○ Call Sally re: Hawaii conference.	○ Plan date night with Eleanor. ○ Invite Stacy and Howie over for dinner. ○ Call Jessica. ○ Be home by 6 to put kids to bed.
Have Fun and Take Care of Myself	**The Other 5%**
○ Go to yoga class.	○ Change oil in car. ○ Buy a new printer. ○ Pay bills. ○ Check out bags for MacBook Air. ○ Call Aly re: her leadership presentation.

This structure helps me carve up my overwhelm into manageable, digestible chunks. And it ensures I'm spending my time where I should. Because saying I want to focus on something is meaningless unless I actually spend my time there. And my to-do list is my plan for where I'm going to spend my time.

But this structure offers more than simplicity and focus and a way to get started. It also offers information about how I'm treating each area of focus, how they stack up relative to one another, and the kinds of things I'm doing to move forward in them.

If you look above, you'll see that, for this particular day, my *Do Great Work with Current Clients* activities far outweigh my *Attract Future Clients* activities. That's fine for a particular day. But if I notice that it's a trend—that for the entire month my current-client work is full and my future-client work is empty—then I know I need to begin to generate activity in that area if I want to move forward and grow my business.

This is particularly useful when trying to decide between two competing demands on your time. If I'm trying to decide between two meetings—both important—I can look at the trend of where I'm spending my time and make the choice based on which area of focus has been lagging. It helps me stay balanced.

On the other hand, my *Have Fun and Take Care of Myself* list also has only one thing in it. But I might decide that it's fine. That between my writing and my family and my friends (all of which give me tremendous energy), I'm getting what I need to take care of myself.

I might also notice that *The Other 5%* is always full, very administratively focused, and taking more than 5 percent of my time. That might be an indication that I should hire an admin person or delay some of those things until I have more time in my schedule.

Fiorella and I worked through her list, putting each to-do item in its category. We realized that many things didn't fit in any of her areas of focus. Which was part of her problem. She was spending time worrying about things that weren't going to get her where she wanted to go, so we culled those. After a few minutes, she had an organized view of what she needed to do and how it was going to move her forward. The fog of overwhelm had dissipated.

She was still frighteningly busy. She still had a tremendous amount to do. But she was no longer frozen. Because she was choosing from six jams, not twenty-four, and was ten times more likely to choose one and start working.

Reduce your overwhelm by putting your tasks in an organized list, focused on what you want to achieve for the year.

23

Wrong Floor

Deciding What Not to Do

I was late for my meeting with the CEO of a technology company and I was emailing him from my iPhone as I walked onto the elevator in his company's office building. I stayed focused on the screen as I rode to the sixth floor. I was still typing with my thumbs when the elevator doors opened and I walked out without looking up, not realizing I had gotten off on the fourth floor instead of the sixth. Then I heard a voice behind me: "Wrong floor." I looked back at the man who was holding the door open for me to get back in; it was the CEO, a big smile on his face. He had been in the elevator with me the whole time. "Busted," he said.

The world is moving fast and it's only getting faster. So much technology. So much information. So much to understand, to think about, to react to.

So we try to speed up to match the pace of the action around us. We stay up until 3 AM trying to answer all our emails. We tweet, we Facebook, and we link in. We scan news websites wanting to make sure we stay up to date on the latest updates. And we salivate each time we hear the beep or vibration of a new text message.

But that's a mistake. The speed with which information hurtles toward us is unavoidable. And it's getting worse. So trying to catch it all is counterproductive.

The faster the waves come, the more deliberately we need to navigate. Otherwise we'll get tossed around like so many particles of sand, scattered to oblivion. Never before has it been so important to be grounded and intentional and to know what's important.

Never before has it been so important to say "no." No, I'm not going to read that article. No, I'm not going to read that email. No, I'm not going to take that phone call. No, I'm not going to sit through that meeting.

It's hard to do because maybe, just maybe, that next piece of information will be the key to our success. But our success actually hinges on the opposite: on our willingness to risk missing some information. Because trying to focus on it all is a risk in itself. We'll exhaust ourselves. We'll get confused, nervous, and irritable. And we'll miss the CEO standing next to us in the elevator.

A study of car accidents by the Virginia Tech Transportation Institute put cameras in cars to see what happens right before an accident. They found that in 80 percent of crashes, the drivers were distracted during the three seconds preceding the incident. In other words, they lost focus—made a call, changed the station on the radio, took a bite of a sandwich, checked a text—and didn't notice that something changed in the world around them. Then they crashed.

And since, in our daily lives, the world around us is constantly changing, we'll almost certainly crash unless we stay focused on the road ahead and resist the distractions that, while tempting, are, well, distracting.

Now is a good time to pause, prioritize, and focus. In the last chapter, "Bird by Bird," we looked at how to structure your to-do list using your five (or so) big things to focus on for the year. That list will help you focus on the road ahead. It will keep your attention on what you are trying to achieve, what makes you happy, what's important to you. That's the list to design your time around.

But we're not done with lists. There's another list that's useful to create: your ignore list.

To succeed in using your time wisely, you have to ask a few more—equally important but often avoided—complementary questions: What are you willing *not* to achieve? What *doesn't* make you happy? What's *not* important to you? What gets in the way?

Some people already have the first list—a to-do list—though there's usually too much on it. Very few have the second—the ignore list. But given how easily we get distracted and how many distractions we have these days, the second is more important than ever. The people who will continue to thrive in the future know the answers to these questions, and each time there's a demand on their attention, they ask whether it will further their focus or dilute it.

Which means you shouldn't create these lists once and then put them in a drawer. These two lists are your map for each day. Review them each morning, along with your calendar, and ask: What's the plan for today? Where will I spend my time? How will it further my focus? How might I get distracted? Then find the courage to follow through, make choices, and maybe disappoint a few people.

After the CEO busted me in the elevator, he told me about the meeting he had just come from. It was a gathering of all the finalists, of which he was one, for the title of Entrepreneur of the Year. This was an important meeting for him—as it was for everyone who aspired to the title (the judges were all in attendance)—and before he entered, he had made two explicit decisions: (1) to focus on the meeting itself; and (2) not to check his BlackBerry.

What amazed him was that he was *the only one* not glued to a mobile device. Were all the other CEOs not interested in the title? Were their businesses so dependent on them that they couldn't be away for one hour? Is either of those messages a smart thing to communicate to the judges?

There was only one thing that was most important in that hour and there was only one CEO whose behavior reflected that importance, who knew where to focus and what to ignore. Whether or not he wins the title, he's already winning the game.

> *To get the right things done, choosing what to ignore is as important as choosing where to focus.*

24

When Tomorrow?

Using Your Calendar

When Eleanor was a little girl, maybe nine or ten years old, she needed new shoes. So she told her mother, and they agreed to go shoe shopping the following Saturday morning. But when Saturday rolled around, Eleanor's mother got too busy and realized she wasn't going to be able to fit in the shoe-shopping trip. So she told Eleanor they'd have to do it later.

"When?" Eleanor asked.

"Sometime this weekend," her mom responded.

"When this weekend?" Eleanor asked.

"Tomorrow," her mom replied.

"When tomorrow?" Eleanor persisted.

"Two in the afternoon," her mom answered.

Eleanor relaxed and smiled. "Sounds great! Thanks, Mom."

And sure enough, at 2 PM the following day, Eleanor and her mom went to buy new shoes. Which, chances are, would not have happened had Eleanor not insisted on knowing exactly when they were going to go.

Eleanor has always been wise, and this is an early example. She intuitively knew what determines the difference between intending to do something and actually doing it. Eleanor understood the secret to getting stuff done.

She reminded me of this a few nights ago when she asked me how my day went and I responded that it went well but many things I'd hoped to do didn't get done. She remarked that I felt that way every night. That I never got to the end of a day and felt like I'd accomplished everything I'd set out to. That, perhaps, what I hoped to get done in a day was unrealistic.

She's right, of course. For many of us, our to-do list has become more of a guilt list. An inventory of everything we want to do, plan to do, think we should do, but never get to. More like an I'm-never-going-to-get-to-it list.

And the longer the list, the less likely we'll get to it and the more stressed we'll become.

We can find the solution to this nightmare in Eleanor's childhood shoe-shopping trip. In the final question that satisfied her: "When tomorrow?"

It's what I call the power of when and where.

In their book *The Power of Full Engagement*, Jim Loehr and Tony Schwartz describe a study in which a group of women agreed to do a breast self-exam. One group was told simply to do it sometime in the next thirty days. The other group was asked to decide when and where in the next thirty days they were going to do it. Only 53 percent of the first group did the breast self-exam. But all of the women who said *when and where* they were going to do it—100 percent—completed the exam.

In another study, two groups of drug addicts in withdrawal (can you find a more stressed-out population?) agreed to write an essay. One group was tasked to write the essay sometime before 5 PM on a certain day. The other group also had to write the essay before 5 PM on a certain day but were asked to first decide when and where on that day they would do it. None of the first group wrote the essay. Not surprising. What is surprising is that 80 percent of those who said *when and where* they would write the essay completed it.

In other words, the problem with typical to-do lists is that we use them as our primary tool to guide our daily accomplishments. But it's the wrong tool. A to-do list is useful as a *collection* tool. It's there to help us make sure we know the pool of things that need to get done. It's why categorizing the list into our areas of focus for the year is so important. Categorizing forces us to pay attention to what's in the pool. It ensures that we're focused on the right things—the ones that will move us forward in what we intend to accomplish for the year.

Our calendars, on the other hand, make the perfect tool to guide our daily accomplishments. Because our calendars are finite; there are only a certain number of hours in a day. As will become instantly clear the moment we try to cram an unrealistic number of things into limited spaces.

So, once you've got your categorized list of things to

do, take your calendar and schedule those things into time slots, placing the hardest and most important items at the beginning of the day. And by "the beginning of the day," I mean, if possible, before even checking your email. That will make it most likely that you'll accomplish what you need to and feel good at the end of the day.

Since your entire list will not fit on your calendar—and I can assure you that it won't—you need to prioritize your list for that day. What is it that really needs to get done today? Which items have you been neglecting? Which categories have you been neglecting? Where can you slot those things into your schedule?

One more thing. As you schedule your priorities on your calendar for the day, make sure to leave some time, preferably in the afternoon, to respond to other people's needs and the items in your *Other 5%* category. If you schedule it, you'll be comfortable *not* doing it until the scheduled time. That leaves you free to focus on your priorities without worrying that you're neglecting anything.

Following this process will invariably leave you with things still on your to-do list that you will not be able to accomplish during the day.

That's a fantastic thing to know ahead of time. Because it would have happened anyway, but you would have ended up surprised, disappointed, and, most important, helpless. Because you were not exerting any real control over what got done and what got left behind.

Now, on the other hand, you can be strategic about

what gets left behind. You can decide, in the morning or the night before, what's really important to get done.

And, like Eleanor and her shoe-shopping trip, you can be relatively certain that if you decide *when and where* you're going to do those things, you'll actually, reliably and predictably, get them done.

> *If you really want to get something done, decide when and where you are going to do it.*

25

The Three-Day Rule

Getting Things Off Your To-Do List

So you've categorized your to-do list. Avoided things that don't fit in with your plan for the year. And made sure that everything on the list reflects where you've strategically chosen to spend your time. Excellent.

Then you've taken your calendar for the day and made hard choices about what you can fit in your limited time. You've decided to do the more challenging things in the morning, when your thinking and patience are at their strongest; and the requests, interruptions, and needs of others can most likely be postponed for later in the day. Perfect.

But that still leaves you with the possibility—or rather probability—of a long list of items that didn't fit into your calendar for the day. And that list will simply grow longer and more stressful—a continued reminder of what you *aren't* accomplishing—day by day. What do you do with those things?

That's where the three-day rule comes in. This rule ensures that no item on your list ever stays on it, haunting you, for more than three days.

Here's what I do: After I've filled my calendar for the day, I review what's left on the list. If there are new items I added that day or the previous two days, I leave them on to see if they make it onto my calendar tomorrow.

But for everything else—anything that's been on my calendar for three days—I do one of four things:

1. **Do it immediately.** I'm often amazed at how many things have been sitting on my list for days that, when I decide to do them, take a few short minutes. Often it turns out to be a thirty-second voice mail or a simple two-minute email. Those things I do immediately.

2. **Schedule it.** If I don't do something immediately, I look for a time to slot it into my calendar. It doesn't matter to me if it's six months away. If it's important enough for me to have on my list, then I need to be able to commit to doing it at a specific time on a specific day. I can always change it when I review my calendar for that day—but if I want it done, it needs to be scheduled.

   There are, of course, some things that I'm not willing to schedule at all. Perhaps a meeting with someone that I think would be a good idea but isn't enough of a priority to schedule. Or something that I schedule and then, each time I get to the scheduled day, I choose to bump off for more-important priorities. If that's the case, then I face the fact that while I'd like to think that particular item is important, I'm not acting that way. So I let it go.

3. **Let it go.** That's a nice way of saying delete the to-do. I simply admit that I will not get done the things I'm not willing to do immediately or schedule for a specific time and day. I face the reality that while I might like them to be priorities, they simply aren't *enough* of a priority to do.

   Sometimes, though, it's too hard to delete something. I simply don't want to admit that I'm not going to do it. Like that meeting. And I don't want to forget that I think someday, maybe, it would be a good idea. So I put those items in a someday/maybe list.

4. **Someday/maybe.** This is a list I got from David Allen, who wrote the bestseller *Getting Things Done*, and it's where I put things to slowly die. I rarely, if ever, do things on this list. I look at it monthly or so, periodically delete the ones that are no longer relevant, and then put the list away for another month. I probably could delete everything on this list, but I sleep a little better knowing I can put things on it when I'm not courageous or guilt-free enough to delete them right off the bat. And who knows? Perhaps someday, maybe, I'll do something on that list.

There's one other list I keep: my waiting list. If I've sent someone an email, left them a voice mail, or expect to hear back from someone about something, I put that item on my waiting list. This way I don't lose track of things I expect from others—and I'm able to follow up if I don't receive them—but I also don't have to look at those items every day or confuse them with things I have to actually *do.* This list is on my computer, and I assign a date and reminder to each item. That way I don't have to think about what I'm waiting for or when I should review the list—I simply wait for the reminder, and if I haven't received the thing I'm waiting for, I'll know to follow up or, as I discuss in a future chapter, let go of the expectation of hearing back from the person.

That's my process. It ensures that nothing stays on my to-do list for more than three days. And once I've scheduled everything I plan to do for the day, I use my to-do list only for details related to things on my calendar (who was that person I was going to call and what's her phone number?) and to add new to-do items that come up throughout the day.

It takes the guilt out of the list.

Never leave things on your to-do list for more than three days. They'll just get in the way of what you really need to get done.

26

Who *Are* You?

The Power of a Beep

Dov is a great guy. The CEO of a professional services firm, he's been successful by any measure. He's financially secure. He's happily married with several children. He's active in his religious community. He's smart, well read, reasonable, and likable. He's the kind of guy you'd enjoy talking with at a dinner party.

Then again, the other day, in anger, he threw a telephone across the room, nearly hitting someone.

"That's not who I am," Dov told me. And it's true. I know him. And I've never remotely experienced him that way.

Now, throwing a telephone is pretty extreme. But if you take it down a notch, Dov is not alone. Lisanne is another incredibly successful leader in a different company— someone whom I personally like and respect tremendously. She's been receiving feedback that she's rude, abrupt, uncommunicative, and harsh. When I discussed the feedback with her, she said the same thing: "That's not who I am."

Dov and Lisanne are, mostly, right. It's not who they are. Usually, anyway. And it's certainly not who they want to be.

But, under the wrong conditions, it *is* who they are. Sometimes.

And it's not just Dov and Lisanne. While most of us would resist the temptation to throw a phone, many of us still manage to lose our tempers more easily than we'd like. The other day, I yelled at my kids—*yelled at them*—for fighting with each other at the breakfast table. I immediately regretted it.

And then, a little later, I was on the line with an AT&T representative, and, after forty-five minutes of getting nowhere, I lost it again.

It's not just anger. We blow people off. Don't return phone calls. Don't pay attention when they're telling us something important. Many of us, at times, act in ways we don't like and don't recognize as ourselves.

I think I've figured out what's causing it: overwhelm.

We have too much to do and not enough time to do it. Which results in two problems:

1. **Things fall through the cracks.** We don't answer all our emails. We don't return all our calls. We don't really listen. And this insults and disappoints others.

2. **We live in a constant state of dissatisfaction.** Feeling ineffective. Feeling insufficient. And so we disappoint ourselves.

In both cases, our tempers get short. Because there's nothing more frustrating than having good intentions and not living up to them. It feels unjust. Like a child who spills something and then cries, "But I didn't *mean* to do it." We don't mean to be mean. But we lose all tolerance for anything that slows us down or that makes demands on us that we can't fulfill. And we get angry at others for our own feelings of inadequacy.

I wasn't angry at the AT&T representative for wasting my forty-five minutes. I was angry at myself for having stayed on the call that long. And I wasn't angry at my kids for fighting as much as I was overwhelmed with cooking waffles and pancakes and oatmeal and setting the table and getting the syrup and the orange juice and making a nice breakfast. But I was so intent on making a nice breakfast that I ruined it.

Planning ahead, knowing what to do and what to ignore, using our calendars strategically: All those are good—and important—daily strategies for managing our day. But we need something more. We need a discipline—a ritual—that can help us stay centered and grounded throughout the day. We need something to remind us who we really are. Who we want to be.

For me, that something is a beep.

Each morning, I set my watch—you can also use a phone, computer, or timer—to beep every hour. At the sound of the chime, I take one minute to ask myself if the last hour has been productive. Then, during that pause, I deliberately commit to how I'm going to use the next hour. It's a way to keep myself focused on doing what I committed to doing.

But, for me, the chime rings deeper than that. When it goes off, I take that deep breath and ask myself if, in the last hour, I've been the person I want to be. In other words, during that pause, I deliberately recommit to not just *what* I'm going to *do*, but also *who* I'm going to *be* over the next hour. It's a way of staying recognizable to myself and to others.

Because if we're going to reverse the momentum, we need an interruption. As soon as I yelled at my kids, I regretted it. Which interrupted my self-defeating behavior.

That interruption was all I needed to remind myself that I was not *that kind* of father. I stopped everything I was doing and sat with them, held them, and apologized for raising my voice.

Wouldn't it be nice if the interruption were a chime rather than a yell? And if it came *before* I lost my temper?

But most likely, your chime won't come at exactly the right time. How many of us lose it exactly on the hour?

It doesn't matter. Because losing control, becoming someone you're not, happens over time. It builds throughout several hours. And that once-an-hour reminder, that one deep breath, that question about who you want to be, keeps you stable. It keeps you *you*.

Maybe your issue isn't losing your temper. Maybe it's multitasking. Maybe it's being so overwhelmed you don't know where to start, so you don't start anything—you just surf the Internet. Maybe it's letting your mind wander while someone is talking to you.

Whatever your issue, when the beep sounds, take a breath and use that one-minute pause to ask yourself whether you're being the person you want to be.

Ask yourself if you're trying to accomplish too much. Or if you're focusing on the wrong things. In other words, disrupt the source that destabilizes you. Reduce the overwhelm. Reconnect with the outcome you're trying to achieve, not just the things you're doing. Then you'll react less and achieve more.

When Dov threw the phone, he immediately regretted it. And he's still working to make up for it. Because, unfortunately, one dramatic disruptive act outside the norm quickly becomes a story that defines the norm.

There is a way to change that story, though. To create a new story. But it's not dramatic. It's deliberate and steady. It's consistent action over time.

We need to remind ourselves of who we know we really are. And then we need to act that way. To be that person. Constantly, predictably, minute by minute and hour by hour.

The right kind of interruption can help you master your time and yourself. Keep yourself focused and steady by interrupting yourself hourly.

27

It's Amazing What You Find When You Look

Evening Minutes—Reviewing and Learning

Julie, the head of a division of a retail company with which I work, was at risk of getting fired. Here's the crazy thing: she was a top performer. She had done more for the brand in the past year than any of her predecessors had in five years.

The problem was that she was a bear to work with. She worked harder than seemed humanly possible and expected the same of others, often losing her temper when they wouldn't put in the same herculean effort she did. She was also competitive and territorial; she wanted the final say on all decisions remotely related to her brand, even when her peers technically had the authority to make them. She wasn't good at listening to others or empowering them or helping them feel good about themselves or the team. And though she was working all hours, things were falling through the cracks.

But none of that was the problem for which she was at risk of losing her job. The real problem was that she didn't think she had a problem. And the reason she didn't think she had a problem was because she was working so hard she never paused long enough to think about it.

I was asked to work with her, and my first step was to interview everyone with whom she worked in order to understand the situation and share their perspectives with her.

When I did share the feedback, her response surprised me. "I didn't know it was that bad," she said, "but it doesn't surprise me." I asked her why.

"This is the same feedback I received at my previous company," she said. "It's why I left."

We could look at Julie and laugh at her ignorance. At her unwillingness to look at her own behavior, at her failures. And to repeat them. But the laugh would be a nervous one. Because many of us—and this includes me—do the same thing.

I'm often amazed at how many times something has to happen to me before I figure it out. I believe that most of us get smarter as we get older. But somehow, despite that, we often make the same mistakes. On the flip side—but no less comforting—we often do many things right but then fail to repeat them.

There's a simple reason for it. We rarely take the time to pause, breathe, and think about what's working and what's not. There's just too much to do and no time to reflect.

I was once asked: If an organization could teach only one thing to its employees, what single thing would have the most impact? My answer was immediate and clear: Teach people how to learn. How to look at their past behavior, figure out what worked and repeat it, while admitting honestly what didn't and changing it. That doesn't mean spending all their time developing their weaknesses. In many cases, what people need to learn is how to leverage their strengths while mitigating the negative impact of their weaknesses. But learning from their past successes and failures is the key to long-term success.

If a person can do that well, everything else takes care of itself. That's how people become lifelong learners. And it's how companies become learning organizations. It requires confidence, openness, and letting go of defenses. What doesn't it require? A lot of time.

It takes only a few minutes. About five, actually. A brief pause at the end of the day to consider what worked and what didn't.

Here's what I propose...

Save a few minutes before leaving the office, before stopping work, or simply toward the end of your day to think about what just happened. Look at your calendar and compare what actually happened—the meetings you attended, the work you got done, the conversations you had, the people with whom you interacted, even the breaks you took—with your plan for what you wanted to have happen. Then ask yourself three sets of questions:

1. How did the day go? What success did I experience? What challenges did I endure?

2. What did I learn today? About myself? About others? What do I plan to do—differently or the same—tomorrow?

3. Whom did I interact with? Anyone I need to update? Thank? Ask a question of? Share feedback with?

This last set of questions is invaluable in terms of maintaining and growing relationships. It takes just a few short minutes to shoot off an email—or three—to share your appreciation for a kindness extended or to ask someone a question or keep them in the loop on a project.

If we don't pause to think about it, we are apt to overlook these kinds of communications. But in a world where we depend on others—and what other world is there?—they are essential.

After several long conversations, Julie came to appreciate the efficiency of slowing down enough to see the others around her. To see that she was working so hard, moving so fast, that even if she was delivering quality results, she was working against herself. Putting her job at risk. And making things harder, not easier.

So over time, she began to change. Slowly and with great effort. But people began to notice. I knew things were going to be okay when I left her a message expecting a call back in several weeks, if at all, but she called me back that evening.

"Hi, Peter," she said. "I just wanted to let you know I

got your call and I appreciate you reaching out to me. I'm heading out with the team for some drinks. I'll try you again in a few days."

And, sure enough, she did.

> *Spend a few minutes at the end of each day thinking about what you learned and with whom you should connect. These minutes are the key to making tomorrow even better than today.*

28

An 18-Minute Plan for Managing Your Day

Creating a Daily Ritual

I started with the best of intentions. I walked into my office in the morning with a vague sense of what I wanted to accomplish. Then I sat down, turned on my computer, and checked my email. Two hours later, after fighting several fires, solving other people's problems, and dealing with whatever happened to be thrown at me through my computer and phone, I could hardly remember what I had set out to accomplish when I'd first turned on my computer. I'd been ambushed. And I know better.

When I teach time management, I always start with the same question: How many of you have too much time and not enough to do in it? In ten years, no one has ever raised a hand.

That means we start every day knowing we're not going to get it all done. So how we spend our time is a key strategic decision. That's why it's a good idea—as we've seen in the last few chapters—to plan ahead, to create a to-do list and an ignore list, and to use our calendars. The hardest attention to focus is our own.

But even with those lists, the challenge, as always, is execution. How can we stick to a plan when so many things threaten to derail it? How can we focus on a few important things when so many things require our attention?

We need a trick.

The late Jack LaLanne, the fitness guru, knew all about tricks; he's famous for handcuffing himself and then swimming a mile or more while towing large boats filled with people. But he was more than just a showman. He invented several exercise machines, including the ones with pulleys and weight selectors in health clubs throughout the world. And his show, *The Jack LaLanne Show*, was the longest-running television fitness program, on the air for thirty-four years.

But none of that is what impresses me. He had one trick that I believe was his real secret power.

Ritual.

Right up until his death at the age of ninety-six, he spent the first two hours of every day exercising. Ninety minutes lifting weights and thirty minutes swimming or walking. Every morning. That ritual enabled him to achieve his goals of staying fit, healthy, and strong. His eleventh book, published when he was ninety-five, was titled *Live Young Forever*.

So he worked, consistently and deliberately, toward his goals. He did the same things day in and day out. He cared about his fitness, and he built it into his schedule.

Managing our day needs to become a ritual, too. A ritual that's simple enough to do each day. Clear enough to keep us focused on our priorities. Efficient enough to not get in the way. And comprehensive enough to incorporate what we've learned in the last few chapters about what works, and what doesn't.

That ritual should take a total of 18 minutes a day:

STEP 1 (5 Minutes): Your Morning Minutes. This is your opportunity to plan ahead. *Before turning on your computer,* sit down with the to-do list you created in chapter 22, "Bird by Bird," and decide what will make this day highly successful. What can you realistically accomplish that will further your focus for the year and allow you to leave at the end of the day feeling that you've been productive and successful? Then take those things off your to-do list and schedule them into your calendar, as we discussed in chapter 24, "When Tomorrow?" And don't neglect chapter 25, "The Three-Day Rule": Make sure that anything that's been on your list for three days gets a slot somewhere in your calendar or move it off the list.

STEP 2 (1 Minute Every Hour): Refocus. Now, remember chapter 26, "Who *Are* You?" Set your watch, phone, or computer to ring every hour and start the work that's listed on your calendar. When you hear the beep, take a deep breath and ask yourself if you spent your last hour productively. Then look at your calendar and deliberately recommit to how you are going to use the next hour. Manage your day hour by hour. Don't let the hours manage you.

STEP 3 (5 Minutes): Your Evening Minutes. At the

end of your day, shut off your computer and review how the day went, asking yourself the three sets of questions listed in chapter 27, "It's Amazing What You Find When You Look." Questions like: How did the day go? What did I learn about myself? Is there anyone I need to update? Shoot off a couple of emails or calls to make sure you've communicated with the people you need to contact.

The power of ritual is in its predictability. If you do the same thing in the same way over and over again, the outcome is predictable. In the case of 18 minutes, you'll get the right things done.

This particular ritual may not help you swim the English Channel while towing a cruise ship with your hands tied together. But it may just help you leave the office feeling productive and successful.

And at the end of the day, isn't that a higher priority?

> *Just 18 minutes a day can save you hours of inefficiency. The trick is to choose your focus deliberately and wisely, and then consistently remind yourself of that focus throughout the day.*

Where We Are

Carefully plan each day ahead. Build each day's plan based on your annual focus. Choose to selectively and strategically ignore the things that get in the way. Use your calendar as your guide and move things off your to-do list. Look back and learn at the end of each day. And, finally, bring it all together by carving out a little time at predictable intervals throughout the day to get and keep yourself on track.

These actions don't take much time. Just a few minutes a day. But they will ensure that you keep getting things done. Not just any things. The right things.

We're not finished yet. In some ways, the next section is the most critical. Because the hardest part of any plan is following through. Withstanding the temptations and distractions that inevitably confront us. Knock us off balance. Or maybe even prevent us from getting started in the first place.

Perhaps the most important skill we can learn is the skill of mastering distraction.

PART FOUR

What Is This Moment About?

Mastering Distraction

It's six in the morning and I'm sitting in my wood-grained and black leather chair, feet on a footstool, laptop on my lap, writing. Getting here, this early in the morning, was not easy. It never is. But without question, it's worth every bit of effort.

I had pressed the FIND ME button, hovered in the air, saw my life, and redirected myself toward where I would make the best use of my strengths, weaknesses, differences, and passions. I chose the areas on which to focus my year, wrote them down, and planned my days around them.

Once I pressed that FIND ME button, my view went from a slowly rotating earth down to my state, my city, my street, and, eventually, to me landing in my chair. The pixels slowly aligned, and my life came into focus. I landed in the perfect place to take full advantage of my particular talents—gifts as well as challenges. Each day, I pour my to-do list into my calendar and watch as my calendar is filled with the right priorities.

I arrived where I am, where I should be, where I can make optimal use of who I am and what I have to offer, by following the ideas in this book.

And yet, for good reason, this book is not over.

Because even when you know where you should focus, and you plan your day around those areas, things get in the way. People call. Emails come in. Things get scheduled for you, sometimes without your even knowing. You get distracted. Sometimes nudged, sometimes knocked, off course.

And it's not just other people getting in our way. Sometimes we get in our own way. Like when we procrastinate on something challenging, something important, perhaps without even knowing why, pushing it off, letting other things take its place.

Most books on time management start too late and end too early. They start with how to manage your to-do items and end with a plan to organize and accomplish all those to-dos.

But that's too late to start because if you haven't made deliberate strategic choices about where you should and shouldn't be spending your time—where you should and shouldn't be spending your life—so that you make the best use of your gifts, then it's likely that many of the things you accomplish will be the wrong things. In other words, you'll waste your time and your life (though you'll be very efficient as you do).

And most time management books end too early

because the hardest part about managing time isn't the plan, it's the day-by-day follow-through: getting started, sticking to your areas of focus, ignoring nonpriorities, and avoiding the allure of unproductive busyness.

Follow-through may seem easy, but it's not. It's where most of us fail. And yet it's the lone bridge across which ideas become accomplishments. We need to follow through, to strongly and diplomatically manage ourselves and other people, so nothing prevents us from accomplishing and becoming all that we can.

I love writing. And it's one of my five areas of focus: *Write and Speak About My Ideas.* But it's hard work, with somewhat flexible deadlines, and tempting to push off for more urgent, easier tasks. In other words, it's a lot easier to decide that writing is important than it is to actually spend time writing. In reality, my writing time is fragile. What I've discovered, after a few missed writing days, is that if I wait until 9 AM or later to start writing, it always slips away, replaced by also-important client work.

This is a struggle that many of us experience all the time. We intend to do something—run in the morning, finish a proposal, have a difficult conversation with someone, stay focused on our plan—but then, in the moment, when it matters most, we get distracted. We don't follow through. We give in.

So now, whenever I can, I schedule my writing to start somewhere between five and six in the morning. At that time, there's little to distract me and I can spend three to four hours writing before the official business day starts.

The best ideas are useless if we can't get started, don't follow through, or get disrupted. The chapters in this section—divided into three parts: *Mastering Your Initiative*, *Mastering Your Boundaries*, and *Mastering Yourself*—offer ideas, practices, tips, tricks, and gentle nudges to get you going, keep you going, and help you create essential boundaries so your actions will move you in the direction you want to go while the distractions simply pass you by.

Mastering Your Initiative

To get anything done, we need the traction to initiate movement from a standstill. In many ways, getting started is the hardest part. I've spent many hours cleaning my house, answering email, surfing the Web, re-sorting my bookshelves, watching television, and eating, eating, eating—in order to avoid a task. Not that eating and cleaning and email aren't worthwhile. But if they're a tactic to avoid what I need—and want—to do, then they're a distraction.

And often, procrastination's strongest influence is at the beginning of a project.

The surprising thing is that many times the task I'm avoiding is actually one I enjoy. And once I get started, I find it hard to stop. But if the task is big and challenging, requiring deep thought and effort, it can feel daunting and I frequently find myself reluctant to start.

The following chapters will help you move through that initial resistance. We'll start by exploring an interesting technique to get things done without needing motivation at all. Then we'll see how, when we do need motivation, we need only a little bit, fun can be a great booster, fear can be a useful kick in the pants, and our thoughts lead the way.

First, let's start by looking at one way to skirt the need for motivation completely.

29

Move the Table

Avoiding the Need for Motivation

I was on an old, rustic train lumbering across the plains of Harambe, Africa (at Disney's Animal Kingdom in Orlando, Florida), when I noticed a majestic lion sitting on a rock on top of a hill, in perfect view.

"Aren't we lucky the lion is out," I mused to the "ranger" on the train with us.

"He's always out there, sitting on that rock," he responded.

"Really?" I said. "How do you get him to stay in that exact spot?"

The ranger just smiled.

Several years ago, I lived in Savannah, Georgia. We moved there from New York City for a variety of reasons, one of which was to enjoy more relaxed outdoor living.

The very first piece of furniture we bought was an outdoor table. Our kitchen had French doors that opened onto a deck that was about six feet square. At the far end of the deck were four steps that led down to a patio garden. It was in that garden that we placed our new table. Our plan was to eat every meal there.

But our plan failed. Maybe we were lazy. Somehow, though, we always chose to eat in the kitchen, where all the food, drinks, plates, and utensils were.

The idea of eating outside was alluring. But the reality was, apparently, too much effort.

Until one day I had a brainstorm. It was an experiment more than anything. I moved the table from the garden to the deck right outside the French doors. The difference was about ten feet and four steps.

After that, we ate *every single meal* outside.

A recent study published in the *American Journal of Public Health* found that the closer teens live to places where alcohol is sold, the greater the likelihood they will binge-drink and drive under the influence.

On a certain level, this may seem obvious. But it's important. Parents tell teens not to drink. Schools tell teens not to drink. Television ads tell teens not to drink. The law prohibits teens from drinking and prohibits liquor stores from selling to teens. And still, if the liquor store is within walking distance of where the teens live (about half a mile), they will be far more likely to drink and drive drunk.

Because, to a larger extent than you probably realize, your environment dictates your actions.

It would be lovely to think that we make our own choices and follow through on them without being too influenced by things around us, but all we need to do is read a little bit of Brian Wansink's book *Mindless Eating* to realize just how much our actions are determined by our environment. Brian did a series of fascinating studies that suggest the reasons we eat have little to do with hunger and a tremendous amount to do with the subtle cues that drive us.

For example, if you use a big spoon, you'll eat more. If you serve yourself on a big plate, you'll eat more. If you move the small bowl of chocolates on your desk six feet away, you'll eat half as much. If you eat chicken wings and remove the bones from the table, you'll forget how much you ate and eat more. If you have a bowl of soup that never gets less than half full, you'll eat more. And the more people you eat with, the more you'll eat.

So don't fight yourself to change your behavior in the midst of the wrong environment; just change the environment. In the case of food, using a salad plate instead of a dinner plate might be all the diet you need.

Marketers already know this. It's why you get so many catalogs over the year. Of course you could go to their website to shop or just use the catalog you already have on the counter. But no, they'll send you another one two weeks before Valentine's Day. And Halloween. And Christmas. They know when you're thinking about buying something and they'll make sure that, just as you have that thought, hey look, a catalog.

If you want to help (or even, dare I say it, manipulate) other people, think about what you want them to do and whether the environment around them supports the behavior.

A client was complaining to me that his receptionist was not warm and friendly with people when they walked in. Guess where the receptionist sat? Think bank teller. That's right. The receptionist sat *behind a glass window*! Don't send her to communication training. Just remove the glass.

A friend of mine, the principal of a school in Boston, wanted to increase student engagement. They should talk to *one another*, he lamented, not just the teacher. He came up with a great solution.

He didn't send out memos. He didn't re-train all the teachers. He didn't print posters and hang them in the classrooms. Instead, he rearranged each classroom, placing the chairs in a semicircle, so the students were facing one another as well as the teacher. Voilà.

If you're leading a team and you want people to talk, knock down the walls. If they sit in ten different countries, use Skype and a video camera permanently attached to their computers so there's no setup time and it's always sitting there, impossible to ignore. It makes a world of difference.

Your goal is to make it *easier to do* something you want done and *harder not to*.

One of my clients wanted everyone in the company to fill out a time sheet, and they were having a very hard time getting people to do it. Their mind-set was *compliance*. They made it very clear that people didn't have a choice. Everyone was *required* to do it. That worked for about half the employee population. The rest simply ignored it.

The leaders were about to send out a memo saying no

one would get paid unless the time sheet was handed in. But wait, I asked, do we know why they aren't doing the time sheet? We assumed it was because people didn't care. But we asked around anyway.

Well, it turns out that people didn't mind the idea of filling out a time sheet, but they were frustrated by the technology. The online system required people to go through a wizard—a series of steps—in order to put their time in. It was meant to help them, but it took longer and needlessly delayed them. Not by much—ten seconds at most—but that was enough to dissuade 50 percent of the people from following through.

Once we changed the form and its technology, everyone started using it. They weren't being defiant. They simply weren't walking the ten feet and four steps to the table. The solution isn't to explain to people why they should take the walk or force them to take the walk. The solution is far simpler: Move the table.

The lion that sat so royally on the rock at the top of the hill, day in and day out, for all the park visitors to see?

It turns out that the rock he sat on was temperature-controlled. It was warm on cold days, cool on hot days. No need to train the lion or tie him to the rock or hope he likes the view. Just make the rock a place he *wants* to sit.

Create an environment that naturally compels you to do the things you want to do.

30

Never Quit a Diet While Reading the Dessert Menu

We Need Less Motivation Than We Think

I woke up one morning to pouring rain and temperatures in the low forties. I had planned on going for an early bike ride in Central Park, but now I wasn't so sure. I like to get some exercise every day, and given my commitments for the rest of the day, this was my only opportunity. But did I really want to get so wet and cold?

I decided to go for it, though I continued to question myself as I put on my biking clothes and got my bike out of the basement. I paused under the awning of our apartment building, as rain streamed down on either side of me.

A friend of mine, Chris, happened to be dashing home to avoid the rain and stopped under the awning for a second.

"Great day for a bike ride," he said sarcastically before running on.

He's right, I thought. *This is crazy.* I stayed under the awning for a few more minutes as I considered retreating into the warmth of my apartment.

Finally, knowing that I'd feel great after a vigorous ride, I got on my bike and took off, pedaling hard. The initial sting of the cold rain had me questioning myself again, but I kept going.

Then, after less than five minutes, the rain stopped bothering me. And after a few more minutes, it felt kind of good. Invigorating. It turned out to be a wonderful ride.

When I got back to the apartment building—drenched, a little muddy, and with a big smile on my face—one of my neighbors commented on how motivated and disciplined I was to be out on a day like that.

But he was wrong. My ride in the rain taught me a good lesson about motivation and discipline: We need it less than we think.

"I didn't need to be motivated for long," I said, laughing. "Just long enough to get outside."

Because once I was already in the rain, it took no discipline to keep riding. Getting started was the hard part. Like getting into a cold pool: Once you're in, it's fine. It's getting in that takes motivation.

In fact, when you think about it, we need to be motivated for only a few short moments. Between those moments, momentum or habit or unconscious focus takes over.

I write a weekly column. Does that take discipline? Sure. But when I break it down, the hardest part—the part for which I need the discipline—is sitting down to write. I'll find all sorts of things to distract me from starting. But if I can get myself to start writing, I don't need much discipline to continue.

Need willpower to work on something difficult? Ask yourself when you need that willpower most. Received feedback that you should talk less in meetings? Figure out when you are most susceptible to blabbing on. Trying to maintain a commitment to yourself or someone else? Identify the times when you are most at risk of violating that commitment.

Then, whatever you do, don't give up in the moments when you're most vulnerable. Don't give up the bike ride while standing under the awning watching it rain. Even when your friend tells you you're crazy.

In other words, never quit a diet while reading the dessert menu. It's too tempting. That's not the right time to second-guess your commitment. It's precisely the time to use your willpower and discipline.

We waste a lot of time, energy, and focus second-guessing ourselves. Am I doing the right work? Is this project worthwhile? Is this employee going to work out? That moment-by-moment deliberation is a distraction at best and sabotage at worst. If you keep asking yourself whether a project is worth working on, you'll reduce your effort on it—who wants to spend time on something that might fail?—and doom its success.

On the other hand, it's impossible to ignore those feelings of uncertainty. The solution? Schedule them. Create an established time to second-guess yourself, a time when you know your commitment won't be weakened by the temptations of the moment. If you're going to break the diet, do it when your need for willpower is at its lowest. Decide to decide the next day, maybe after a healthy breakfast or a little exercise, when you know your inclination to stick to your goals will be naturally high.

Then, if you decide to stay on the diet, commit fully and powerfully until the next scheduled time to deliberate. Knowing you have a planned pause allows you to focus and concentrate without hesitation until the established time to second-guess yourself.

And if you do eventually decide to change your commitment, you'll know it's not from momentary weakness. It'll be a strategic, rational, intentional decision.

What's important is that your moment of choice is when you are in the right state of mind—when you need the least willpower—to make the best decision.

You need to be motivated for only a few seconds. Know when you're vulnerable and you'll know when you need to turn it on.

The Nintendo Wii Solution

Having Fun

When my friend Richard asked me to join him in training for a triathlon, I carefully considered his request. For about a second.

"No way."

"Oh, come on. Why not?"

"Because I've raced triathlons before. They're painful. It takes me a week to recover. And for what? It's—"

"Wait a second," Richard interrupted. "Do you actually try to win?" He laughed. "Peter, last year there were fifty-seven people in my age-group. I came in fifty-sixth. Right before the guy with one leg." Then he looked me up and down. "You know, we're not the kind of guys who win these races."

"So why do you do it?" I asked.

"It's fun."

Research published recently in the *Annals of Behavioral Medicine* showed that the harder people exercise, the less pleasure they feel during the exercise and the less likely they'll be to exercise routinely. As Panteleimon Ekkekakis, one of the authors of the study, said in *The Wall Street Journal*, "Evidence shows that feeling worse during exercise translates to doing less exercise in the future."

Obvious, right? We tend to do things we find pleasurable and avoid things we find painful. But we often forget the obvious as we try to push to get things done. Efficiency, it turns out, is the enemy of fun. And yet in the end, fun is so much more efficient than efficiency.

"Look," someone complained to me about one of her colleagues, "he's an adult. I tell him to do something, he should do it. I don't care whether he wants to or not. It's his job. It's why he's paid."

But that's not how things really work.

Everything I've seen confirms a simple rule: People do what they choose to do. And if something's fun, they'll choose to do it.

Marc Manza is the chief technology officer of Passlogix, a client of Bregman Partners. A few years ago, Marc had a problem. Passlogix's software was conflicting with an older, unsupported version of Sun Microsystems software that some of their clients were still using. Marc wanted to work with Sun to fix the problem, but Sun simply told Marc to tell his clients to upgrade to the newer version of Sun software.

So Marc had his team work on a fix. But it was complicated, and two years later, at a cost Marc estimates in the tens of thousands of dollars, the problem remained unsolved.

Then one day Marc had an idea. He went to a local electronics store, bought a Nintendo Wii, and placed it in a central, visible place in the office. Then he made an announcement: The first person to solve this problem wins the Nintendo. And he added a rule: You have to work on the problem on your own time, not on company time.

It took two weeks.

Marc took a boring project working on a legacy system and made it fun. Cost to the company? Two hundred and fifty dollars.

Since then he's given away iPods, Xbox 360s, Play-Station3s, and a netbook. Fun competitions that solve real problems are a great way to boost morale and keep people engaged, especially in somewhat depressing times. This is true whether we're motivating other people or ourselves. Two rules:

1. **Focus on real problems and opportunities.** A company picnic might be fun, but it doesn't achieve the same impact. Instead, make the work itself fun. One way to do this is to get others involved. Solving problems with other people is often more fun than solving them alone.

2. **Money isn't fun.** When Marc put a $1,000 bounty on a problem, it failed. The cash could have bought four Nintendos, but it was less inspiring. You can parade around the office with a box in your arms as a badge of honor, but who would walk around waving a check? Getting paid for something transforms fun into work. Fun is not about the money.

Special projects that require creativity to crack are the most fun to attack. Like figuring out how to get the attention of a new prospect who won't return calls. Or solving a product issue that consistently annoys customers. Or finding a new way to communicate with your manager or employee without relying on the dreaded performance review.

But mundane tasks can be made fun, too. Take the anxiety-producing cold call. What if you started a running list (with a prize for the monthly winner) of the most obnoxious responses you hear? That alone could turn angst into excitement.

Fun doesn't require a competition. When I was waiting tables as a college student, I spiced up the job by serving each table in a different accent. It took all my focus to remember which accent went with which table. Silly? For sure. Fun? Much more so than simply taking an order.

Here's the thing, though: You can't fake fun. Which means you have to go into your workday with a sense of amusement. It's a lens through which you view the world. We all know people who slip easily into laughter and make jokes even as they work hard at something, seemingly unburdened by the threat of failure. And when they do fail, they laugh and keep going. It's contagious. Which is why it's such a critical leadership quality.

Fun keeps us motivated in a way that eventually translates into performance. After one of his races, Richard called to tell me he came in 120th out of 200, a huge improvement over previous races. "And they all had two legs," he told me, laughing. "Wanna join me for the next one?"

Sounds like fun.

> *Fun reduces our need to motivate ourselves because fun is motivating.*

32

The One-Two Punch

Getting Started and Keeping It Going

I was on my cell talking with someone about something—I can't remember who or what anymore—as I ushered my three children toward our minivan, parked across the street from our apartment building.

I held the phone in my right hand and several bags in my left as I struggled to keep the kids from running into the street. Daniel, my two-year-old, was holding on to my pant leg as Sophia and Isabelle—four and eight—saw the van across the street and started to run to it.

"Wait!" I screamed before they launched themselves off the sidewalk. They stopped just in time to avoid a car that sped by. My adrenaline shot up as I realized the close call. I should have gotten off the phone at that point—it's obvious now—but I didn't. I thought I had averted the disaster.

It's amazing what it takes to change a person's behavior.

I continued to talk on the phone as I led the kids across the street and into our car.

I got into the driver's seat, turned the ignition, and put the car in reverse, twisting around to look behind me, still on the phone. "Get your seat belts on," I whispered, trying not to interrupt my call as I slowly moved the car back.

That's when the car's sensor system began beeping, signaling there was something behind me.

I looked out the back window but didn't see anything. So in my rush, still on the phone, gesturing to the kids to put on their seat belts and moving the car slowly in reverse, I ignored the signal. Even as the beeps got closer together.

Suddenly the car jolted and I heard a crash.

I slammed on the brakes and finally—because that's what it took—got off the phone. I walked around to the back of the car and saw two fallen, mangled motorcycles.

I could have noticed them when I got in the car or seen them in the rearview picture that appears on my GPS screen or stopped when the beeps sounded.

But I was too distracted.

The thing that really freaks me out is that those motorcycles could have had riders on them. Or they could have been children playing.

I got off easy. No one was hurt. But thankfully, I was shaken.

Driving while talking on a cell phone is the equivalent of drunk driving. And texting is worse: People who text behind the wheel are twenty-three times more likely to get into an accident because, a recent study shows, a driver sending or receiving a text message spends 4.6 of every 6 seconds with his eyes off the road.

Those seconds of distraction—the glance at the phone, the almost imperceptible moment of inattention—are the difference between avoiding an accident and creating one.

Here's what's interesting: You already know this. We all do.

And yet we still do it.

In fact, we do all sorts of things we know are destructive in the long run. Like eating ice cream when we're trying to lose weight. Or arguing to prove we're right when it doesn't matter. Or answering email while on a phone call.

So why don't we stop? What's so hard about not talking on a cell phone while driving? Or stopping an argument before it's too late?

Amazingly, we think we can get away with it. Because—and I'm not excluding myself here—we lack imagination.

Sure, we think, *other people get into accidents while on their cell phones. But it hasn't happened to me yet. And given my experience of driving and calling without crashing, it's hard to really imagine that it will.* So we keep on talking and driving.

Well, if lack of imagination is the problem, amplifying our imagination and experiencing it in the present could be the solution.

There's an ongoing argument in the world of behavior change: What works better—reward or fear, carrot or stick, hopeful vision or burning platform? Some argue you need both at the same time.

My experience is that you need both but not at the same time. If you want to change behavior, start with fear, then experience the reward. It's the one-two punch. The jab and the follow-through.

Fear is a great catalyst. It's the booster rocket, the initial push that moves us through the atmosphere of inertia.

I—and more than 3.5 million other people—watched a four-minute YouTube video dramatizing an accident caused by a teenage girl who was texting while driving. The video shows the gory details of the crash and its aftermath.

I watched the girl, blood covering her face, as she stared in anguish at her friends—whom she had killed—in the seats around her. I felt her pain. Her regret. Her devastation.

After seeing that video, I stopped using my cell phone in the car. Watching it had given me an experience of my potential future self. I could imagine—and even feel—what it might be like if it had been me driving that car.

What's so useful about fear is that it's a current experience of a future possibility. Even if what we fear is in the future, we feel the fear now. And since our decision making favors current experience, we're willing to change our behavior to reduce the fear.

I have a friend who wants to lose weight and, in a moment of honesty, suggested that she'd (almost) like to have diabetes so she would be forced to eat more healthfully. Fear is a tremendous motivator.

But it doesn't last. I hate to admit it, but within a few days of mangling the motorcycles, and a few days after watching the video, I was back to talking on my cell while driving.

Because fear is unsustainable. It's exhausting and stressful and destructive over time. Its purpose is short-term change. For long-term change, the experience of fear needs to be followed by the experience of a better life.

That's the second step. The reward. The fulfilled promise of a better present. The nourishment that keeps us going for the long-term.

When I realized that, I watched the video again (a nice booster shot of fear) right before a long drive with my family. Then I paid attention to how it felt to drive without distraction. I got into a groove. I settled in. I enjoyed the driving itself. I had a great conversation with Eleanor. It turned out to be the nicest drive I had experienced in a long time.

Start with fear. Then notice—pay close attention to—the positive impact of your choice.

If you want to lose weight, shut your eyes before taking the first bite of ice cream and imagine, for a brief second, what you would look like if you were twice your current size. Think about how you might get diabetes. Really visualize it. Exaggerate it even. That's your stimulus. The spark plug that will start your engine of change.

And then after a few days, as you begin to feel healthier, more energetic, you can let go of that fear and hold on to the feeling of a looser belt.

In the middle of that argument—the one in which you insist on being right when it doesn't matter—pause for just a moment to imagine people wanting to avoid future conversations with you. Picture them making an excuse and walking away. Call to mind your performance review with their comments on it. Really see it in the moment. That fear will help you stop.

Then let go of those fear-inducing images and make sure to pay attention to the changing quality of your conversations, the pleasure of other people's company, and your own reduced stress.

That—like the calm, cell-phone-free drive—is the reward that will sustain the change you've made.

Fear can be a useful catalyst to change—then pleasure sustains it. If you need help getting yourself going, don't choose one or the other. Choose one before the other.

33

Am I the Kind of Person Who...

Telling the Right Story About Yourself

I was walking back to our apartment in Manhattan, the hood of my jacket pulled tight to keep the rain out, when I saw an older man with a walker struggling to descend the slippery stairs of his building. When he almost fell, I and several others went over to help.

There was an Access-A-Ride van (a Metropolitan Transit Authority vehicle for people with disabilities) waiting for him. The driver was inside, warm and dry, as he watched us straining to help his passenger cross the sidewalk in the pouring rain.

Then he opened the window and yelled over the sound of the rain coming down, "He might not be able to make it today."

"Hold on," we yelled (there were five of us now) as we helped the man move around the back of the van, "he can make it."

Traffic on Eighty-fourth Street had stopped. We caught

the man from falling a few times, hoisted him back up, and finally got him to the van door, which the driver then opened from the inside to reveal a set of stairs. The man with the walker would never make it.

"What about your side door, the one with the electric lift?" I asked.

"Oh yeah," the driver answered. "Hold on." He put his coat over his head, came out in the rain with the rest of us, and operated the lift.

Once the man with the walker was in safely, we'd all begun to move away when the driver opened the window one more time and yelled, "Thanks for your help."

So here's my question: Why would five strangers volunteer to help a man they don't know in the pouring rain—and think about the electric lift themselves—while the paid driver sat inside and waited?

Perhaps the driver is simply a jerk? Perhaps. But I don't think so. Once we suggested the lift, he didn't resist or complain; he came outside and did it immediately. And he wasn't obnoxious, either. When he thanked us for our help, he seemed sincere.

Maybe it's because the driver is not permitted to leave the vehicle? I actually checked the MTA website to see if there was a policy against drivers' assisting passengers. On the contrary, it states: "As long as the driver doesn't lose sight of the vehicle and is not more than 100 feet away from it, the driver can assist you to and from the vehicle, help you up or down the curb or one step, and assist you in boarding the vehicle."

So why didn't the driver help? Part of the answer is probably that for him, an old man struggling with a walker isn't a onetime thing, it's every day, every stop, and the sight doesn't compel him to act.

But that answer isn't good enough. After all, it's his job to help. That's when it suddenly hit me: The reason the driver didn't help might be precisely because he was paid to.

Dan Ariely, a professor at Duke University, and James Heyman, a professor at the University of St. Thomas, explored this idea. They set up a computer with a circle on the left side of the screen and a square on the right side, and asked participants to use the mouse to drag the circle into the square. Once they did, a new circle appeared on the left. The task was to drag as many circles as they could within five minutes.

Some participants received $5, some 50 cents, and some were asked to do it as a favor. How hard did each group work? The $5 group dragged, on average, 159 circles. The 50-cent group dragged 101 circles. And the group that was paid nothing but asked to do it as a favor? They dragged 168 circles.

Another example: The AARP asked some lawyers if they would reduce their fees to $30 an hour to help needy retirees. The lawyers' answer was no. Then AARP had a counterintuitive brainstorm: They asked the lawyers if they would do it for free. The answer was overwhelmingly yes.

Because when we consider whether to do something,

we subconsciously ask ourselves a simple question: *Am I the kind of person who . . ?* And money changes the question. When the lawyers were offered $30 an hour their question was, *Am I the kind of person who works for $30 an hour?* The answer was clearly no. But when they were asked to do it as a favor? Their new question was, *Am I the kind of person who helps people in need?* And then their answer was yes.

So what does this mean? Should we stop working for money? That wouldn't be feasible for most people. No, we need to get paid a fair amount, so we don't say to ourselves, "I'm not getting paid enough to..."

Then we need to tap into our deeper motivation. Ask ourselves: Why are we doing this work? What moves us about it? What gives us the satisfaction of a job well done? What makes us feel good about ourselves?

The same holds true for motivating others. People tend to think of themselves as stories. When you interact with someone, you're playing a role in her story. And whatever you do, or whatever she does, or whatever you want her to do, needs to fit into that story in some satisfying way.

When you want something from someone, ask yourself what story that person is trying to tell about herself or himself, and then make sure your role and actions are enhancing that story in the right way.

We can stoke another person's internal motivation, not with more money, but by understanding, and supporting, his or her story. "Hey," the driver's boss could say, "I know you don't *have* to get out of the van to help people, but the fact that you do—and in the rain—that's a great thing. And it tells me something about you. And I appreciate it and I know that man with the walker does, too." Which reinforces the driver's self-concept—his story—that he's the kind of guy who gets out, in the rain, to help a passenger in need.

Ultimately, someone else's internal motivation is, well, an internal issue. But there are things we can do that will either discourage or augment a person's internal drive. And sometimes it's as simple as what we notice.

And what's true about someone else is true about you. What's your story about yourself? How would you finish the sentence "I'm the kind of person who..."? And how does that story support—or detract from—what it is you want to accomplish?

It's not lost on me that I, too, have a story about myself—I'm the kind of guy who stops on a rainy day to help an old, disabled man to his van—and that it makes me feel good to tell you about it. That will make it more likely that I'll do it again in the future.

As we left the scene, I looked at the drivers of the cars who waited so patiently and waved, mouthing the words *thank you* as they passed. Every single one of them smiled back. Wow. New York City drivers smiling after being stuck in traffic for ten minutes? That's right.

Yeah, they were thinking behind their smiles, *I'm the kind of driver who waits patiently while people less fortunate than me struggle.*

A good story—one you feel deeply about and in which you see yourself—is tremendously motivating. Make sure the story you tell about yourself (sometimes only to yourself) inspires you to move in the direction you want to move.

34

The Hornets Stung My Mind

Getting Out of Your Own Way

While visiting her parents in North Carolina, Eleanor and I escaped for a few hours to go mountain biking in Panthertown Valley. Several times during our ride, we stopped to admire the incredible views and warm our faces in the sun. *The perfect day,* we thought.

As we coasted down the last few feet to the parking lot, we had to squeeze through the space between a tree and a short but wide metal post. Eleanor made her way first, leaned on the post for balance, and then glided down toward the car. My turn. I reached out for the post and paused, watching Eleanor.

Suddenly I felt stabbing pain everywhere. Little blades piercing my body. All over my arms and legs, on my back, through my clothing. It was a second or two before I heard the buzzing, felt the brushing, and realized what was happening. By then it was too late. Hornets. A swarm of them. The post I was holding was hollow, and inside was their nest. Eleanor must have rustled them up when she passed.

I sprang off my bike and ran, flailing, thrashing about, slapping myself until it seemed like the hornets had gone. I was covered in stings, about a dozen of them.

Then the dreaded question: Was I allergic? I hadn't been stung since I was a boy, when I'd had a mild reaction. What would it be like now, especially with so many stings? Would my throat swell up? Would I stop breathing?

The nearest pharmacy was fifteen minutes away. The nearest hospital twenty-five. We threw the bikes onto the car and drove off. The stings were red and swelling. I sensed a lump in my throat. It was hard to take a deep breath. Was my fear getting the better of me? Or was I going into anaphylactic shock? Eleanor drove faster.

The mind is an amazing tool. We can use it to think through complex problems and intuit subtle emotions. We can dream up dazzling ideas and make them happen.

But occasionally, our minds just take over. We imagine the worst, feeding our fear with fantasies and, sometimes, creating a future that fulfills our nightmares.

Charles, a senior leader, was convinced he was being driven out of his company. When he wasn't invited to a meeting, was left off an email list, or was told his work could be improved, he saw it as proof of a plot to discredit him.

Charles spoke with his boss, the CEO, but she didn't see it. You're doing a good job, she told him, I value and respect you. But it didn't help.

When he was left out of another meeting, one to which his boss was invited, he took it as evidence that she was sidelining him, too. Now it was clear to him that everyone—his colleagues, his own direct reports, even his boss—was trying to push him out.

"Your boss doesn't have to try to push you out," I reasoned with him. "She's the CEO. She could just fire you if she wanted." Of course, that didn't help, either.

His boss asked him to meet with her, planning to tell him he was achieving his goals and doing well. But Charles vented for twenty minutes about how everything he did got twisted, subverted, and manipulated.

The CEO left the meeting thinking there was no solution except to fire him.

Charles didn't simply confirm his fears, he manifested them. His mind envisioned a world and then created it. He isn't paranoid or schizophrenic or crazy. He's just human.

We do this all the time. We think someone is angry with us, so we respond aggressively to a gesture and they become angry with us. See? We were right all along. We think a customer isn't going to give us business, so we don't pursue them, and they don't renew our contract. We knew it! Our neglect was justified.

What can we do about it?

As Einstein said, we can't solve a problem by using the same thinking that created it. In this case we can't solve the problem using any thinking at all. Because thinking is the problem. And sometimes it's virtually impossible to change our thinking. Better just to stop thinking altogether. But what should we do instead?

Pretend. Act *as if*.

When the CEO called Charles into her office, he should have listened, thanked her, and, defying everything he thought was happening to him, acted *as if* he were a valued member of the team. Then, the next time he wasn't invited to a meeting, he should have asked to be invited, saying he'd like to help with the project at hand. Because that's what a valued member of the team would do.

What should you do with someone you think is angry at you? Ask them about it. If they say they're not angry, then act *as if* they're telling the truth. Respond generously to anything they do. Pretend you believe they meant well.

An unresponsive customer? If they say they want to meet with you but they're just busy, then choose to believe them. Keep calling.

Will you be living in a fantasy world? Maybe. But you might already be living in one. Why not choose the fantasy that works for you instead of against you?

The mind is so hard to control that sometimes, when it runs off in rampant fear or anger or frustration, you shouldn't try. Just accept that it might be playing tricks on you and invent a work-around.

As the hornet stings turned into red blotches and welts, I wasn't controlling my fear that I was going into shock. The harder I tried, the worse I made it.

So I gave up. Instead of focusing on the possibility that I

might be allergic, I reminded myself that I had been stung before with only a mild reaction. *Sure*, my mind responded, *but you've never been stung this many times at once.* I shut my eyes, took a deep breath, and decided there was no difference.

And then, knowing it's impossible to *not* think about something, I distracted myself by talking to Eleanor about a dinner we were planning for that night. Crazy as this sounds, I simply acted *as if* there were no danger from the stings.

We continued to drive to the pharmacy—it would have been reckless not to. But by the time we arrived, my mind had relaxed, my breathing had improved, the lump in my throat was gone, and the adrenaline had receded. It was almost as if I had not been stung at all.

> *Your mind can help you move forward or can get in the way. Choose the fantasy world that supports you.*

Where We Are

The sooner we get started in making valuable use of our time, the more fully we'll live our lives. And, as we've seen, getting started doesn't have to be hard. We can design our environment so it naturally impels us toward our goals. Once we realize that it only takes a second to get going, we can simply will ourselves through procrastination. Or we can make the task so fun that we won't feel hesitant at all. If that doesn't work, then a little fear, a good story, or the productive use of our imagination can all help.

Once we've gotten going, though, we'll face a whole new challenge: the distractions set before us by others.

Mastering Your Boundaries

So you've gotten started on your worthwhile, important work. You know it's worthwhile and important
because it was on your to-do list under one of your
areas of focus for the year. Then, during your morning minutes, you moved it from your to-do list to your
calendar. And now you're working on it.

You're already much further along than most
people. You're headed in the right direction. But don't
relax yet. Because there are well-meaning people—
nice, polite, sincere people—who are out to get you.
Seductive sirens who want to tempt you away from
your effort.

They're not malicious, but they need your attention. And, sometimes, you need to give it to them.
At other times, though, they're simply a distraction you can't afford. How can you tell the difference? And what should you do when you figure it
out? The chapters in this next section will offer some
guidance, rules, and advice on how to master your
boundaries so you can resist the distractions set
before you by others, starting with how to know
when you *should* tend to the requests people make
of you.

When should you say yes to someone? When

and how should you say no? When should you confront someone? What are some things you can do to help others use your time wisely? What are the right boundaries to set? These are some of the questions we'll explore in the following chapters.

35

The Time Suck of Collaboration

Saying Yes Appropriately

Nate started working for a large consulting firm after many years as an independent consultant. He called me for some advice shortly after joining the firm.

"I'm wasting a tremendous amount of time," he complained to me. "I'm in meetings all day. The only way I can get any real work done is by coming in super-early and staying super-late."

Nate had gone from an organization of one to an organization of several thousand and was drowning in the time suck of collaboration. He is not alone.

I surveyed the top 400 leaders of a 120,000-person company and found that close to 95 percent of them—that's 380 out of 400—pointed to three things that wasted their time the most: unnecessary meetings, unimportant emails, and protracted PowerPoints.

Working with people takes time. And different people have different priorities. So someone may need your perspective on an issue that's important to him but not to you. Still, if he's a colleague, it's important to help. And often, we want to help.

On the other hand, we've all felt Nate's pain. The question is: How can we spend time where we add the most value and let go of the rest?

We need a way to quickly and confidently identify and reduce our extraneous commitments, to know for sure whether we should deal with something or avoid it, and to manage our own desire to be available always. I propose a little test that every commitment should pass before you agree to it. When someone comes to you with a request, ask yourself three questions:

1. Am I the right person?
2. Is this the right time?
3. Do I have enough information?

If the request fails the test—if the answer to any one of these questions is no—then don't do it. Pass it to someone else (the right person), schedule it for another time (the right time), or wait until you have the information you need (either you or someone else needs to get it).

Ideally, it's best not to be interrupted. But sometimes an interruption will be important and appropriate. For example, what if your boss is the person who interrupts you? Or what if you're on vacation and a critical client reaches out with a time-sensitive and crucial question?

These three questions offer a clear, easy, and consistent

way of knowing when to respond, so you can resist the temptation to respond to everything.

If your boss asks you to do something and her request fails the test, it's not just okay—it's useful—to push back or redirect so the work is completed productively. It's not helpful to you, your boss, or your organization if you waste your time on the wrong work.

That's the irony. We try to be so available because we want to be helpful. And yet being overwhelmed with tasks—especially those we consider to be a waste of our time—is exactly what will make us unhelpful.

When we get a meeting request that doesn't pass the test, we should decline. When we're cc'd on an email that doesn't pass the test, we need to ask the sender to remove us from the list before we get caught up in the flurry of REPLY ALL responses. And a fifty-page presentation needs to pass the test before we read it (and even then, it's worth an email asking which are the critical pages to review).

A few weeks after sharing the three questions with Nate, I called him at his office at around 6 PM to see how it was going. I guess it was going well, because I never reached him. He had already gone home.

Resist the temptation to say yes too often.

36

But Daddy . . .

Saying No Convincingly

I was in my home office, on the phone with a new client, when I heard a knock on the door. I looked at my watch: It was 4 PM, the time my daughters, Isabelle and Sophia, come home from school. Generally I love taking a break at this time and hearing about their day.

But I have a rule: If the door to my office is closed, they have to knock once. If I answer, they can come in. If I'm silent, it means I don't want to be disturbed and they have to wait until I come out.

Well, this time, not wanting my call to be unprofessionally interrupted, I remained silent. But they kept knocking and, eventually, just walked in. I was stunned! What about my rule? I signaled for them to be silent but let them stay in the room until the call was over.

After my phone call, I asked them why they had disobeyed my rule.

"But Daddy," Isabelle said, "you like when we just come

in. We did it yesterday and the day before and you didn't say no."

I had broken the cardinal rule of rules: *Never break a rule*.

I should know better. Just a few days earlier, after a speech I had given about time management to the top leaders of a large pharmaceutical company, one leader, Sean, approached me with a question. How could he stop his secretary from interrupting him?

"I'll have the door shut and Brahms playing on the stereo—I mean, how much more obvious can I be?—and she'll walk in and ask me a question. It doesn't seem like a big deal, but it's a distraction, and it throws me off. I tell her not to, but she does it anyway."

Sean is already ahead of the game. He realizes something most of us miss: It's hard to recover from an interruption. In a study conducted by Microsoft Corporation, researchers taped twenty-nine hours of people working and found that, on average, they were interrupted four times per hour. That's not surprising.

But there's more, and this part is surprising: Forty percent of the time they did not resume the task they were working on before they were disrupted. And it gets worse: The more complex the task, the less likely the person was to return to it.

That means we are most often derailed from completing our most important work.

"So," I asked Sean, "what do you say when she interrupts you?"

"I remind her that I told her I didn't want to be disturbed."

"Great. Then?"

"Then she tells me it will just take a second and asks me a question or talks to me about an issue."

"And?"

"Well, I already stopped doing what I was doing before and I don't want to seem mean or rude, so I give her what she needs and then ask her not to disturb me again."

That's Sean's mistake. And mine. And perhaps, if you find that people don't always do what you ask, yours, too. We like being liked. We're too nice. We don't want to appear rude.

Unfortunately, it's a bad strategy. Because setting a rule and then letting people break it doesn't make them like you—it just makes them ignore you.

If Sean wants his secretary to listen to him, he needs to be consistent; no exceptions. On the other hand, he also needs to understand why she's constantly disturbing him. Sean travels and is often out of his office, so his secretary is never sure when she will have the opportunity to connect with him. But when he's in the office, she knows she can reach him. She's not being obnoxious. On the contrary, she's being diligent.

To solve his problem and stop the interruptions, Sean needs to do two things:

1. Set a regular appointment—that he does not cancel— to meet with his secretary to address any questions or open issues.

2. When she does interrupt him, and she will, he needs to look at her without smiling and tell her that what-ever it is, it needs to wait until their appointed time.

"And if it's a short question? Like: What time is your lunch appointment today?" Sean challenged me.

"I know it's hard. Silly even. But do not answer her. Just tell her you cannot be disturbed and let the silence sit there. If you want her to respect the rule, she needs to see that you won't break it. Even if maybe, in that situation, it makes sense to break it. It's a slippery slope."

As Sean listened to me, he shuddered slightly at the thought. "That will be very uncomfortable," he finally said.

"That's the point," I told him. "You want it to feel uncomfortable. You want *her* to feel uncomfortable. That's what will prevent her from interrupting you again."

Later, if he wants, he can explain that his work requires total concentration and even a small interruption will cause him to lose his train of thought. But not at the time. Because an explanation at the time will reduce the discomfort.

Think of it this way: Ultimately, people feel safer know-ing what the boundaries are. It may seem harsh at the time, but in the long run it reduces their stress and uncertainty. People prefer to know where they stand.

"You're right," I told Isabelle after she called me on my inconsistency. "It's hard not to break my own rule because I love seeing you guys so much. But the rule really is impor-tant and I can't break it again."

The next day I was working on the computer when, as

expected, Isabelle and Sophia knocked and then walked in without waiting for my response.

I turned to look at them. "I adore you guys. But I'm working now. Whatever it is, it needs to wait until I'm done," I said.

"But Daddy..."

"Sorry," I repeated.

"But we just..."

"Sorry, I can't be disturbed now," I said once more, feeling like a jerk. I wanted to see them. I even worried for a second that they really needed me. What if one of them was hurt? What if there was a fire in the kitchen? But I didn't look up. My wife was home. If there was a fire, she would put it out. She's very good at that.

A few days later, they tried again, but I didn't waver. And they haven't broken the rule since.

They learned that when I said no, I meant it. And eventually, they came to respect my boundary.

When you say no, mean it, and you won't need-lessly lose your time.

37

The Third Time

Knowing When to Say Something

Should I bother to have the conversation with her? What do you think?" Mike, a marketing director, was telling me about Lorraine, one of his employees, who had done a few things to frustrate him. She arrived late to a meeting with a client. Not that late—only ten minutes. Still, it didn't look good.

Then, a few days later, she was supposed to email him some information by 4 PM and didn't do it until 6 PM. I know, he told me, not a big deal. He didn't really need it until the next morning. Still.

And then, not long after, he received a voice mail from her saying she wouldn't be able to make a conference call they had planned with a colleague in another office. The call was an internal matter. Nothing time-sensitive. But she didn't give him a reason, and that bothered Mike.

"None of these things are a big deal," Mike told me,

"and she's a great employee. But I'm annoyed. Should I say something or shrug it off?"

Trying to decide whether to talk to someone about something is a surprisingly time-consuming activity. Should we? Shouldn't we? Maybe we talk to three other people to ask their advice—which takes more of our time and their time.

So I have a rule for dealing with these types of situations—times when I'm not sure if it's worth raising an issue. I need a rule, because it's often hard to know if something's a big enough deal to address until it's too late and then, well, it's too late. It's already gotten out of hand. On the flip side, if I jump on every single issue the first time it comes up, then, well, *I'll* be out of hand.

So the first time someone does something that makes me feel uncomfortable, I simply notice it. The second time, I acknowledge that the first time was not an isolated event or an accident but a potential pattern, and I begin to observe more closely and plan my response. The third time? The third time I always speak to the person about it. It's my rule of three.

If someone makes a joke about my consulting rates— maybe they say something like, "well, with rates like those, it's a good thing you add value (chuckle, chuckle)"—I might laugh along with them but I notice my discomfort. The second time, I smile but don't laugh. The third time I say, "This is the third time you've joked about my rates—I know it's a joke, but I also wonder if you feel that they exceed my value. If so, I'd like to talk about it with you."

If you come late to a meeting once, I notice. Three times? I bring it up.

The first time you demonstrate a lack of teamwork, I notice. The third time? I need to better understand your commitment to the group.

I always say some version of, "I've noticed something three times and I want to discuss it with you." That way we both know it's a trend.

Is it okay to talk to them about it the first time? Sure. You don't have to wait. But everyone slips once or twice. Just don't let it go more than three times without having a conversation. Three is a good rule of thumb because it allows you to act with confidence that it's not all in your head. And in these situations, confidence is critical to your ability to speak with authority.

"So," Mike said to me after I explained my rule of three, "are you saying I should talk to her about it?"

"I can't help but notice you've asked me that same question three times," I said. "What do you think?"

Don't wait too long to bring something up. People can only respect boundaries they know are there.

38

We're Not Late *Yet*

Increasing Transition Time

At 6 PM, Eleanor was looking tense. "We are so late!" she said.

After a great day of skiing in the Catskills, we were driving back to New York City for a dinner party that was called for 7 PM.

"What do you mean?" I responded. "The party doesn't start for an hour. We've got plenty of time."

"Peter." She didn't hide her annoyance. "We're a hundred miles from the city. There's no way we can make it on time."

"But we're not late *yet*." I smiled. "We're still an hour early."

This explains why I am always late and Eleanor is always on time. Eleanor, you see, plans for transition time.

The night before the party, she figured out that if we needed to be there by 7 PM, we should plan to arrive by 6:45, which meant leaving our apartment in New York City at 6:15, which meant arriving at the apartment by 5:30, in time to drop off our bags, take showers, and dress, which meant arriving in New York City at 5 to give us time to park the car, which meant leaving Windham ski mountain at 2:15, in case there was traffic, which meant stopping skiing at 1:15, giving us time to pack up and clean the house, which meant starting skiing at 8 in the morning if we were going to get in any decent runs, which meant waking up at 6:30, which meant going to sleep by 10:30 so we could get our full eight hours.

"Uh-oh," I had said to her the night before as I looked at my watch. "It's eleven o'clock. We're already thirty minutes late for tomorrow night's party."

Eleanor, of course and as usual, is right. The only way to get somewhere on time is to plan for it, taking into account each time-consuming step.

My intentions are good. I don't like being late. Most people who are late don't *like* being late. And I never *plan* to be late or *intend* to be late. I understand that it's disrespectful and unprofessional. Not to mention uncomfortable.

Here's my problem: I have a very high need to be efficient and productive. And transition time is neither of those things; it's annoying.

I'd rather just *be* somewhere. I don't want to waste the time *getting* there. So even though I know I should leave more time, I push it, clinging to the illusion that I can get places faster than is humanly possible.

I'm not the only one. Anyone who has ever scheduled

back-to-back meetings lives under the same illusion. How can we end a meeting at 2 PM and start the next one at 2 PM? Even if they're just phone meetings, we can't dial that fast. Or switch our mind-set from one task to the other in so little time. And when you throw in a bathroom break? It's premeditated lateness, and we do it all the time.

One of my clients has a *policy* not to start a training program until ten minutes after it is scheduled to start. That's institutionalized lateness.

But the joke is on us late people. Because being late causes the exact things we're trying to avoid: inefficiency and counterproductivity. Not just for the people who are waiting, but for the people who are late. Because nothing is more productive and efficient than transition time. It's not just our time to travel. It's our time to think and to plan.

How many meetings have you attended in which, halfway through, you begin to wonder: *Now, what is the point of this meeting?*

How many times have you been on a phone call and found your mind wandering, or—be honest now—surfed the Web, because you were bored?

How often have you thought: *You know, this sixty-minute meeting should have been thirty minutes?*

And you're right. The meeting probably should have been thirty minutes. Or forty-five at the most. Because almost anything that could be done in sixty minutes can be done in forty-five. But since we haven't thought enough about it beforehand, the meeting drags on.

If we took a few minutes before the meeting to really

think about it, we could drastically shorten it. So here's the one thing you should think about as you transition leisurely (gasp) to your next commitment:

How can I make this shorter, faster, and more productive?

Even five or ten minutes of that kind of planning can shave thirty minutes off a task. Think about your outcome. Think about what you really need from people. And then, in a move that will make everyone else in the room overjoyed, let them know you want to make the sixty-minute meeting thirty minutes and tell them how you plan to do it.

Spend your transition time plotting how to maximize your outcome. Need people's ownership? Think about how you can involve them more openly, get their perspectives, and engage them. Going to a dinner? Ponder how you can have more fun.

Maybe you're thinking, *But I already plan.* Sure you do. But there's no better planning time than the fifteen minutes before you walk into the room or get on the phone. Do you know any athlete who would rush off her cell phone and jump into the starting gate of a race? Of course not. Because athletes know that transition time is productive time.

To make this work, we need to schedule it—literally put the transition time on our calendars. End meetings at least fifteen minutes before the hour and schedule that time to prepare for the next one. Maybe, then, we can keep that meeting to thirty minutes and have an extra fifteen minutes to go to the bathroom, answer email, or surf the Web. That would be more efficient than doing those things during the meeting.

I have more to say about this. But it's only fifteen minutes until my next meeting so I've got to go. And besides, it's 4 PM, and by my calculations I'm already running late for a 2 PM meeting tomorrow.

A few moments of transition time can help make your next task shorter, faster, and more productive for you and others.

39

I Don't Want to Go to Ski Class

Decreasing Transition Time

I don't want to go to ski class!" Sophia, my daughter who was four years old at the time, was crying. I knelt down on the snow so we could be at eye level and asked her why.

"I just don't want to go," she whimpered.

I didn't want her to skip class. She was already skiing well—turning and stopping on her own—so I knew she could do it. Plus, she'd asked for lessons, and we'd committed with the instructor. I wanted to teach her that she needed to follow through on her commitments. Finally, I had seen this before: She'd cried while learning to ride a bicycle, but when she finally learned, she was tremendously proud of herself.

I tried to comfort her, reason with her, convince her that, in fact, she liked class, and at the end of it she would smile and tell me she had fun.

But she was still crying when we walked up to her ski teacher. She hugged me, then hugged me again. I walked away, but when I heard her continue to cry, I came back and hugged her more, telling her again how the class would help her ski better, how she would have fun, how it wouldn't be so bad.

Finally, after twenty minutes of trying to comfort her without success, I tore myself away.

Later that morning, I was on the chairlift with two teenagers and their mother. I asked the mother what she would do in my situation.

She didn't hesitate. "Drop 'em and run!" She laughed. "Remember?" She looked at one of her sons. "I would put you on the floor at day care and ten seconds later you could hear the tires screeching as I pulled away."

Now we were all laughing, and I realized she was right. My mistake? I prolonged the agony.

In the last chapter, I extolled the virtues of transition time, arguing that if we only built in a little extra time before a meeting, call, or event, we could use that time to prepare.

It's incredibly valuable when the transition time is used to make the subsequent activity more useful, more productive, maybe even shorter.

But in some situations, transition time isn't the solution. It's the problem. As long as Sophia was in the transition, she was miserable. And by trying to comfort her through it, I prolonged her misery. I kept her in the pain of the transition.

We do this in organizations all the time. We decide on a change and then spend a tremendous amount of energy trying to get everyone to feel great about it before they have a chance to experience it. We try to get them to want it.

But sometimes, too much preparation can be a bad thing.

Imagine you're on a cliff overhanging a river, and you've decided you're going to jump into the water. Would you be better off standing at the edge, looking down, convincing yourself it will be okay? Or would you be better off just jumping without thinking about it?

Sometimes it's better to shut your eyes and jump. Especially if you feel anxious about your next step.

I know a large company that moved offices from New York City across the Hudson River to New Jersey over a period of a year, a move many people were dreading. Some departments opted to move immediately to secure space and get it over with, while others stayed in New York City as long as possible, trying to delay the pain.

The delaying strategy backfired. The departments that stayed in New York started to feel the pain right away—in their anxious anticipation of the move—and continued to feel it right up until they actually moved. Then the pain continued for a few months until they adjusted to their new reality.

The departments that moved early started their adjustment period right away, cutting out many months of trepidation. The reality of being in New Jersey just wasn't as bad as people feared.

When we fear something, we often complain about it. And when we complain about something, we rile ourselves up and convince ourselves that our fears are justified. The more we complain about a decision that's already been made, the more frustrated we become. And the more we resent being in the situation.

So if there's something you need to do that you find difficult—writing a proposal, having an unpleasant conversation with someone, or doing any work you consider unpleasant—try doing it first thing in the morning so you minimize the time you have to think about it.

And if you're in a position to help others through a transition? Here are three steps that may quicken the transition:

1. **Listen fully to their concerns.** Repeat back what you hear them saying and ask if you got it right. Once they agree that you understand their issues, move to step 2.
2. **Share your perspective. Once.** Check for their understanding, not their agreement. You want to make sure they hear your view.
3. **Don't repeat.** This is the critical step to moving them through the transition to the other side. If you've performed steps 1 and 2 effectively, you're done. Any more just lengthens the transition—and the dread.

I knew Sophia was going to class, so I needed to move her out of contemplating the change and into living it as quickly as possible. I should have hugged her and left.

"She cried for the first few minutes of class," her ski teacher told me at pick up, "but then she was fine."

I knelt down to Sophia and asked her how she liked it. She stared at me intently, looking angry, like she was about to cry again.

We stayed like that for several seconds, looking at each other without saying anything. Her face remained stern. Then she broke into a wide smile. "It was fun," she said, and fell into my arms.

When you shorten transition time, you create a boundary that helps you and others adjust to a new reality.

40

We'll Regress. We'll Forget You. We'll Replace You.

Managing the Tension of Relaxation

Every time I go on vacation, I feel two distinct emotions: excitement and anxiety.

Anyone who knows me knows how much I adore my family and the time we spend together. And that includes stuff like changing diapers and putting groggy kids back to bed at four in the morning. Fun or not, I treasure it.

Still, vacation makes me anxious because I know I'll feel torn. When I'm not working, I'll feel like I should be; and when I am, I'll feel like I shouldn't be.

Some will accuse me of being a workaholic. But it's not just that, and it's not just me. We live in a world in which we're expected to be available all the time for almost any reason. Worse, we expect it from ourselves.

Leashed to our technology, we find it harder to spend an unadulterated moment doing anything. Forget about vacation. How about a short break in *conversation*? We quickly check our email. A walk from one office to another? Check voice mail. Bathroom break? I hate to say it, but it's rare to walk into a men's room and not see a man at a urinal with one hand on his BlackBerry (the other hand, well, I'm not looking).

Sure, we might say we have no choice. But while non-stop work might feel overwhelming, it's also reassuring. It makes us feel busy. Valuable. Indispensable.

Unfortunately, there's a downside to feeling indispensable. And going on vacation brings that downside up. You can't get away. Or you won't.

Because getting away—truly not being needed for a week or two—raises all sorts of insecurities.

Two years ago, after ten years of running my company, I took a month off and went to France with my family. As I prepared to leave, I spoke with each of my clients, letting them know I'd be away. One client, Ross, the CEO of a small company and also a good friend, smiled at me, his eyes twinkling.

"It'll be okay," he said. "Just know that three things will happen: We'll regress. We'll forget you. And we'll replace you." Then he laughed. Ha-ha.

I laughed, too, and then quickly added, "Of course, you know I'll be reachable if you need me."

Ah, there's the rub. Reachable if needed. And since we all like to be needed...

There are two reasonable ways to deal with this problem without ruining a vacation by staying plugged in 24/7.

1. **Completely unplug.** I've done this a few times when
   I was literally unreachable—for example, when I
   spent a week camping and kayaking down the Grand
   Canyon. And while I find this close to impossible to
   do unless I am forced, it was a wonderful break.

   When I returned to civilization—and a phone—
   I had more than fifty messages. But here's what I
   found most interesting: The first half of the messages
   all raised problems that needed to be resolved, and
   the second half were the same people telling me
   not to worry about the first half because they had
   resolved the problems on their own.

   It turns out that unplugging created an opportunity for my team to grow, develop, and exercise
   their own judgment. Still, for some of us, unplugging
   completely might not be realistic. Which brings us to
   option two...

2. **Schedule plug-ins.** Choose a specified time—and
   time frame—each evening when you will be reachable. A few minutes at the end of each day (or, if you
   can manage, every few days) to answer emails and
   make phone calls.

   Of course, before you schedule the time, you
   need to admit to yourself that you will work during
   the vacation. But setting aside some time to work
   means you're setting aside the rest of the time to not
   work. And that just might save your vacation.

This strategy is a good one even when you're not on vacation, though the plug-ins will be more frequent. Scheduling specific time to take care of emails and phone calls each day avoids the technology creep that takes over so much of our lives. It allows us to concentrate on a single thing for longer without getting interrupted.

Scheduling time sets clear expectations—for you, for the other people on your vacation, and for the people reaching you. Everyone will be relieved.

Thankfully, when I came back from my month away, Ross's company had not regressed. They didn't forget me, and they didn't replace me. Next time, when I leave for vacation, I'm sure I'll bring my laptop. I still want to be reachable if someone needs me. But only for half an hour a day.

When you take vacation—or any other time you want to be undisturbed—schedule a specific time to take care of the things that would otherwise creep into each and every available moment.

Where We Are

Knowing when to say yes and how to say no. Knowing when to confront someone and how to draw boundaries with them and, in many cases, with yourself. That sets the foundation to master distractions set before you by others.

Still, there's a harder set of distractions to master: the distractions you can't blame on anyone else. The distractions you create yourself.

Mastering Yourself

Even when we're working alone, behind closed doors maybe, with no one to distract us, somehow, someway, we're often able to find creative ways to distract ourselves. Maybe it's the allure of an incoming email. Or the overwhelming desire for perfection that subverts our efforts to stick with hard work when it looks ugly. Maybe we're working hard, but the effort doesn't seem to be producing results, and we're not sure what to do differently, so we feel the almost overwhelming urge to quit.

These are common distractions we experience whenever we try to accomplish something meaningful and demanding. Thankfully, a few tools of thought can help us maintain our commitment—and follow through—when we're tempted to give up.

In the following chapters, we'll see how distracting ourselves could, in some situations, be useful, while multitasking is just about always useless. Then we'll explore how being productive and half right is better than being perfect and never ready. And how flexibility might be the most important skill of all.

First, though, it's important to recognize that not all distractions are bad. In fact, sometimes the best way to combat distracting interruptions is to create a few productive ones yourself.

41

Does Obama Wear a Pearl Necklace?

Creating Productive Distractions

The screaming started a few minutes before breakfast. As far as I could tell, our two-year-old son, Daniel, took our then-seven-year-old daughter Isabelle's markers from her while she was drawing. And if you don't think that's a big deal, then you don't have kids.

I tried my typical parenting monologue: "I can see you're very upset; he's two years old, sweetie, and he doesn't know any better; the picture is beautiful just as it is; you needed to stop drawing anyway, it was time for breakfast; you have lots of other markers; okay, that's enough—stop crying." Nothing worked.

And then I recalled some research I had read.

"Isabelle," I asked, "is that a new T-shirt you're wearing?"

"Yes," she said, still crying.

"Who's that on the front?"

She looked at her shirt. "Obama." She wasn't crying now.

"What? No way. It's a woman! Does Obama wear a pearl necklace?" I asked.

She laughed.

The research I recalled was the famous marshmallow experiment conducted on four-year-old children in the 1960s by Walter Mischel, a professor of psychology at Stanford University. He put a marshmallow on a table in front of a child and said he needed to leave the room for a few minutes. The child was welcome to eat the one marshmallow while he was gone, but if he or she could wait until he returned, he would give the child two marshmallows. Then he left, and the hidden video camera captured the rest.

Dr. Mischel was interested in what enabled some children to delay gratification while others surrendered to it. Most kids succumbed in less than three minutes. Some, however, made it the full twenty minutes until the researcher returned. And as it turns out, they were rewarded with more than just an extra marshmallow. As follow-up research later discovered, these kids had better relationships, were more dependable, and even scored an average of 210 points higher on their SATs than the children who couldn't resist the marshmallow.

So what's the secret of the ones who held out? Did they have more willpower? Better discipline? Maybe they didn't like candy as much? Perhaps they were afraid of authority?

It turns out it was none of these things. It was a technique. The same technique I used with Isabelle.

Distraction.

Rather than focusing on not eating the marshmallow,

they covered their eyes, sat under the table, or sang a song. They didn't resist the urge. They simply avoided it.

We face two challenges as we try to manage our behavior: the challenge of initiative (exercise, make one more sales phone call, work another hour on that presentation, write that proposal), and the challenge of restraint (don't eat that cookie, don't speak so much in that meeting, don't yell back, don't solve your employee's problem for him).

If we're good at the challenge of initiative, it means we're good at applying ourselves, at focusing, at breaking through resistance using sheer willpower. In other words, we're good at avoiding distraction.

Which, as the experiments show, is exactly what leads us to fail in the challenge of restraint. Focusing on resisting the temptation only makes it harder to resist. In the case of not eating the cookie, using willpower only makes it more likely that we'll eat the cookie. Or speak too much in the meeting. Or yell back.

Try this experiment: For the next ten seconds, don't think about a big white elephant. Go ahead. Try it. Just make sure you don't think about a white elephant.

Impossible, right? The trick is to distract yourself by focusing on something else entirely.

The rule is simple: When you want to do something, focus. When you don't want to do something, distract.

Distraction has a bad rap. It's seen as something that prevents you from achieving your goals. We *get* distracted.

Focus, on the other hand, is seen as positive and active—something you do to achieve your goals.

But the skill of distraction is important now more than ever. We are living in an age of fear—terrorism, global warming, child kidnappings, a volatile economy—that reduces our productivity at best and destroys our health, relationships, and happiness at worst.

Unfortunately, the more we feel afraid, the more we read about the source of our fear as we try to protect ourselves. Afraid of losing your job or your nest egg? Chances are you're following the market closely and reading more articles about the economy than ever before. According to a recent poll released by the National Sleep Foundation, one-third of Americans are losing sleep over personal financial concerns and the poor condition of the U.S. economy.

The solution? Distraction. Read a great book. Watch a movie. Play with a four-year-old. Cook and eat a meal with good friends. Go for a walk. Throw yourself into work.

Distraction is, in fact, the same thing as focus. To distract yourself from X you need to focus on Y.

The CEO of a midsize company complained to me about Phillip, one of his direct reports, a senior leader who was micromanaging his team.

"Does Phillip have any particular passions you know about?" I asked.

"The environment," he responded.

I asked him if that issue was also important to the company, and he said it was.

"Great," I said. "Start a task force to address environmental issues and opportunities at the company, and ask Phillip to lead the effort."

He looked worried. "Won't that distract him from his day-to-day responsibilities?"

I smiled. "I hope so."

Distraction, used intentionally, can be an asset.

42

Would You Smoke Pot While You're Working?

Avoiding Switch-Tasking

I was on a conference call—the executive committee of a not-for-profit board on which I sit—and decided to send an email to a client.

I know, I know. You'd think I'd have learned.

In chapter 32, "The One-Two Punch," I wrote about the dangers of multitasking—using a cell phone while driving—and I proposed a way to stop.

But right now I wasn't in a car. I was safe. At my desk. What could go wrong?

Well, I sent him the email. Then I had to send him another one, this time with the attachment I had forgotten to append. Finally, my third email to him explained why that attachment wasn't what he was expecting. When I eventually refocused on the call, I realized I hadn't heard a question the chair of the board had asked me. I swear I wasn't smoking anything.

But I might as well have been. A study showed that

people distracted by incoming email and phone calls saw a ten-point fall in their IQ. What's the impact of a ten-point drop? The same result as losing a night of sleep. More than twice the effect of smoking marijuana.

Doing several things at once is a trick we play on ourselves, thinking we're getting more done. In reality, our productivity goes down by as much as 40 percent, because we don't—and can't—multitask. We switch-task. Rapidly shifting from one thing to another, interrupting ourselves unproductively, losing time in the process.

You might think you're different. That you've done it so much you've become good at it. Practice makes perfect and all that.

But you'd be wrong. The research shows that heavy multitaskers are less competent at it than light multitaskers. In other words, in contrast to almost everything else in your life, the more you multitask, the worse you are at it. Practice, in this rare case, works against you.

So I decided to experiment for a week. No multitasking. I wanted to see what happened, which techniques helped, and whether I could sustain it.

For the most part, I succeeded. When I was on the phone, all I did was the phone. In a meeting, I did nothing but focus on the meeting. Any interruptions—email, phone, a knock on the door—I held off until I finished what I was working on.

When I emerged at the end of the week, I discovered six things:

First, it was delightful. I noticed this most dramatically

when I was with my children. I shut my cell phone off and found myself much more deeply engaged and present with them. I never realized how significantly a short moment of checking my email disengaged me from the people and things right there in front of me. Don't laugh, but I actually—and for the first time in a while—noticed the beauty of leaves blowing in the wind.

Second, I made significant progress on challenging projects. The kind that require thought and persistence. The kind I usually try to distract myself from, like writing or strategizing. Since I refused to allow myself to get distracted, I stayed with them when they got hard, and experienced a number of breakthroughs.

Third, my stress level dropped dramatically. The research shows that multitasking isn't just inefficient, it's also stressful. And I found that to be true. It was a relief to do one thing at a time. I felt liberated from the strain of keeping so many balls in the air at each moment. It felt reassuring to finish one thing before going to the next.

Fourth, I lost all patience for things I felt were not a good use of my time. An hour-long meeting seemed interminably long, and a meandering, pointless conversation was excruciating. In other words, I became laser-focused on getting things done. Since I wasn't doing anything else, I got bored much more quickly. I had no tolerance for wasted time.

Fifth, I had tremendous patience for things I felt were useful and enjoyable. When I listened to Eleanor, I was in no rush. When I was brainstorming a difficult problem, I stuck with it. Nothing else was competing for my attention, so I was able to settle into the one thing I was doing.

Sixth, and perhaps most important, there was no downside. Nothing was lost by not multitasking. No projects were left unfinished. No one became frustrated with me for not answering a call or failing to return an email the second I received it.

Which is why it's surprising that multitasking is so hard to resist. If there's no downside to stopping, why don't we all just stop?

I think it's because our minds move considerably faster than the outside world. You can hear far more words a minute than someone else can speak. We have so much to do, why waste any time? While you're on the phone listening to someone, why not use that extra brainpower to book a trip to Florence?

What we neglect to realize is that we're *already* using that brainpower to pick up nuance, think about what we're hearing, access our creativity, and stay connected to what's happening around us. What we neglect to realize is that it's *not* extra brainpower. It may be imperceptible, but it's all being used, right then and there, in the moment. And diverting it has negative consequences.

So how do we resist the temptation to multitask?

First, the obvious: The best way to avoid interruptions is to turn them off. Often when I'm writing, I'll do it at 6 AM. when there's nothing to distract me. I'll disconnect my computer from its wireless connection, and I'll turn my phone off. In my car, I'll leave my phone in the trunk. Drastic? Maybe. But most of us shouldn't trust ourselves.

Second, the less obvious: Use your loss of patience to your advantage. Create unrealistically short deadlines. Cut all meetings in half. Give yourself one-third the time you think you need to accomplish something.

Because there's nothing like a deadline to keep things moving. And when things are moving fast, we can't help but focus on them. How many people run a race while texting? If you truly have only thirty minutes to finish that presentation you thought would take an hour, are you really going to answer that call?

Interestingly, because multitasking is so stressful, single-tasking to meet a tight deadline will actually reduce your stress. In other words, giving yourself less time to do things could make you more productive *and* more relaxed.

Finally, it's good to remember that we're not perfect. Every once in a while, it might be okay to allow for a little multitasking. As I was finishing this chapter, Daniel, my two-year-old son, walked into my office, climbed on my lap, looked up at me with a smile, and said, "I want to watch *Monsters, Inc.,* please."

So here we are. I'm writing this sentence on the left side of my computer screen while Daniel is on my lap, watching a movie on the right side.

Sometimes, it really is simply impossible to resist a little multitasking.

> *We don't actually multitask. We switch-task. And it's inefficient, unproductive, and sometimes even dangerous. Resist the temptation.*

43

It's Not the Skills We Actually Have That Matter

Getting Over Perfectionism

According to the World Database of Happiness (yes, there is one), Iceland is the happiest place on earth. That's right, Iceland. Yes, I know it's cold and dark six months out of the year there. I'm just giving you the data.

The secret to their happiness? Eric Weiner, author of *The Geography of Bliss*, traveled to Iceland to find out. After interviewing a number of Icelanders, Weiner discovered that their culture doesn't stigmatize failure. Icelanders aren't afraid to fail—or to be imperfect—so they're more willing to pursue what they enjoy. That's one reason Iceland has more artists per capita than any other nation. "There's no one on the island telling them they're not good enough, so they just go ahead and sing and paint and write," Weiner writes.

Which makes them incredibly productive. They don't just sit around thinking they'd like to do something. They do it. According to the psychologist Mihaly Csikszentmihalyi, who wrote the book *Flow: The Psychology of Optimal Experience*, "It is not the skills we actually have that determine how we feel but the ones we think we have."

So if you *think* you're good at something, whether or not you are, you'll do it. The converse is also true: If you think you aren't good enough at something, you won't do it.

Now, some of you naysayers will be thinking, *Wait a second, didn't Iceland go bankrupt?* And you naysayers are right. There are some times—some things—in which failure can't be tolerated. The financial system of a country is a good example. So is heart surgery. But for the majority of the projects we work on? Failure can be a good sign. It means you got started.

A friend of mine, Raphael, has wanted for some time to start a business teaching guitar. But he hasn't yet. Why? When you sift through his various explanations and excuses, it comes down to one simple problem.

He's a perfectionist.

Which means he'll never think he's good enough at guitar to teach it. And he'll never feel that he knows enough about running a business to start one.

Perfectionists have a hard time starting things and an even harder time finishing them. At the beginning, it's they who aren't ready. At the end, it's their product that's not. So either they don't start the screenplay, or it sits in their drawer for ten years because they don't want to show it to anyone.

But the world doesn't reward perfection. It rewards productivity.

And productivity can be achieved only through imperfection. Make a decision. Follow through. Learn from the outcome. Repeat over and over and over again. It's the scientific method of trial and error. Only by wading through the imperfect can we begin to achieve glimpses of the perfect.

So, how do we escape perfectionism? I have three ideas:

1. **Don't try to get it right in one big step. Just get it going.** Don't write a book, write a page. Don't create the entire presentation, just create a slide. Don't expect to be a great manager in your first six months, just try to set clear expectations. Pick a small, manageable goal and follow through. Then pursue the next.

   These smaller steps give you the opportunity to succeed more often, which will build your confidence. If each of your goals can be achieved in a day or less, that's a lot of opportunity to succeed.

2. **Do what feels right to you, not to others.** Eleanor is a fantastic mother to our three children. Their sleep is extremely important to her, and in her early days of parenting, she read a tremendous number of parenting books, each one with different advice on how to predictably get children to sleep through the night. Each expert contradicted the next.

   The only thing those books succeeded in doing was to convince her that she didn't know what she was doing. It was only after throwing all the books away that she was able to find herself as a parent. It's not that she found the answer. In fact, what helped was that she stopped looking for *the* answer.

What she found was *her* answer, and that allowed her to settle into her parenting. It made her calmer, more consistent, more confident. And that, of course, helped our children sleep better.

By all means, read, listen, and learn from others. But then put all the advice away, and shoot for what I consider to be the new gold standard: good enough.

Be the good-enough parent. The good-enough employee. The good-enough writer. That'll keep you going. Because ultimately, the key to perfection isn't getting it right. It's getting it often. If you do that, eventually, you'll get it right.

3. **Choose your friends, co-workers, and bosses wisely.** Critical feedback is helpful as long as it's offered with care and support. But the feedback that comes from jealousy or insecurity or arrogance or without any real knowledge of you? Ignore it.

And if you're a manager, your first duty is to do no harm. A friend of mine, Kendall Wright, once told me that a manager's job is to remove the obstacles that prevent people from making their maximum contribution. That's as good a definition as I've ever heard.

And yet, sometimes, *we* are the obstacle. As

managers, we're often the ones who stand in judgment of other people and their work. And when we're too hard on someone or watch too closely or correct too often or focus on the mistakes more than the successes, then we sap that person's confidence. Without confidence, no one can achieve much.

Catch someone doing seven things right before you point out one thing they're doing wrong. Keep up that seven-to-one ratio, and you'll keep your employees moving in the right direction.

These three ideas are a good start. Don't worry about following them perfectly, though. Just well enough.

> *The world doesn't reward perfection. It rewards productivity.*

44

Why Won't This Work for You?

The Value of Getting Things Half Right

There's very little these days that we accomplish by ourselves. Most of the time, we have partners, colleagues, employees, friends, clients, associates—and the list goes on—with whom we work. And more often than not, our ability to get things done is, in part at least, dependent on their willingness and drive to get things done.

So to get them on board, we create lengthy presentations to make a convincing case—and we lose our audience. Or we hold long meetings to gain buy-in—but our bored colleagues end up spending the time on their Black-Berrys. Maybe we try to get good visibility by copying lots of people on our emails, but instead they simply delete them, and us, as irrelevant.

Because none of that stuff works. In fact, it works against us.

There are times in life when I expect something to be just right. Perfect. Like when I open the box of my new

MacBook Air, for example. Or when I take money out of the ATM.

In most cases, though, I expect imperfect. And when working with others, I think that's a good thing—but not in the if-I-expect-imperfect-I-won't-be-disappointed sense.

I'm not suggesting you *settle* for imperfect. I'm advising you to *shoot* for it.

Several years ago, a large financial services company asked me to help them roll out a new performance management process for two thousand people.

"Why me? Why not do it yourselves?" I asked my prospective client. This might seem strange coming from a consultant, but I always think companies are better off doing things themselves if they can.

"We tried!" she responded with exasperation. "We identified the standards we expect from people. We created the technology system in which to write the reviews. We sent out lots of communication. We practically wrote the reviews for them. But they're not doing it. After two years of training people, we still have only a 50 percent rate of completion. Now we're looking into whether we can give people a bonus for doing reviews—"

"Wait," I said, interrupting her. "You're going to pay managers *extra* to talk to their employees?"

She looked a little embarrassed.

"Give me six months," I said.

When I reviewed the materials, I was impressed, even intimidated. They had paid meticulous attention to detail. Not only in *what* they gave their employees (the materials looked beautiful), but also in *how* they tried to get people to use the system.

They followed all the rules of traditional change management. They had sponsors (senior-level people who spoke about the importance of performance management). They had change agents (people whose job it was to make sure that everyone was committed to the change). They had time lines, communication plans, and training programs.

Still, only half the managers were completing their reviews.

I assembled my team: fifty people spread out across three continents. I redesigned the materials, the training, the messages. Then I began the roll-out, right on schedule.

It was a complete and utter failure. People resisted. They complained. My own team dissented.

So I pushed harder. After all, I'd designed this myself. It was *perfect*.

And that's when it hit me. *Of course* I thought the performance review process was perfect. I'd created it. I would be more than happy to use it. But I wasn't the person who needed to use it. Here's what I figured out:

1. My perfect is not their perfect.
2. *They* don't have a perfect. In fact, there is no *they*. There are two thousand individuals, each of whom wants something a little different.
3. The more perfect I *think* it is, the less willing I'll be to let anyone change it.

4. The only way to make it useful to *everyone* is to allow *each person* to change it to suit him- or herself.
5. The only way people will use it is if they *do* change it in some way.
6. The only way I will encourage them to change it and make it their own is if I make it *imperfect.*

So I stopped the roll-out immediately. And I changed everything to make it half right, half finished. It wasn't pretty, but it was usable.

Even the trainings were half designed. Halfway through each training, after describing the process, I always asked the same question—a question people were more than happy to answer:

Why won't this work for you?

"There are too many standards on this form. I don't have that much to say about my employees, and it will take too much time."

I responded to every answer with the same response:

That's a good point. So how can you change it to make it work?

"I guess I could just fill out the standards that apply to that employee." *Great.*

"Three people who don't report to me are asking me to review them, and I have nothing to say about them."

That's a good point. So how can you change it to make it work?

"I can redirect the review to the appropriate manager." *Great.*

"There's no standard here that relates directly to the issue my employee is having."

That's a good point. So how can you change it to make it work?

"I'll just write in the standard I think is appropriate." *Great.*

One by one, we dealt with all the issues people saw as obstacles. One by one, they made their own changes. One by one, they took ownership for the system and became accountable for using it.

Is this only a large-scale change idea? Not at all. It's useful whenever you need someone else to take ownership for something. Just get it half right.

Hiring someone new? Get the job description half right and then ask her: *Why won't this work for you?* When she answers, you respond: *That's a good point. So how can you change it to make it work?* She'll look at you a little funny because, after all, you're the boss and you should be telling her what to do. Then you'll just smile and wait for her to answer and the two of you will redesign the job right there, right then. No better time or place to send the message that she is accountable for her own success.

Delegating work to someone? Give him the task and then ask: *Why won't this work for you?* When he answers, you respond: *That's a good point. So how can you change it to make it work?*

Here's the hard part: When someone changes your plan, you might think the new approach will be less effective. Resist the temptation to explain why your way is better. Just

smile and say *Great*. The drive, motivation, and account-
ability that person will gain from running with her own
idea will be well worth it.

This doesn't just work internally. It's also a great way to
make a sale. Get the pitch half right and then say...you
guessed it... *Why won't this work for you?* Then go ahead
and redesign the offer in collaboration with your potential client. You'll turn a potential client into a collaborative
partner who ends up buying his own idea and then working with you to make it successful.

Forget about lengthy presentations and long meetings.
During economic downturns, when it is critical to get more
done with fewer resources, getting things half right will
take you half as long and give you better results.

How did this work in the performance review roll-out?
One year later, the numbers came in: Ninety-five percent of
managers had done their reviews.

Imperfectly, I expect. Which, of course, is the key.

> ***Don't settle for imperfect. Shoot for it.***

45

Don't Use a Basketball on a Football Field

Staying Flexible

I was driving in the mountains in upstate New York when I found myself in a sudden snowstorm. It was hard to see, the road was slick, and I could feel the wind pushing my car around. I was scared.

I thought about pulling over and waiting it out, but I had no idea how long it would last. So I kept going, but realized I needed to drastically change my driving. I slowed down, put on my hazards, turned off the radio and phone, and inched my way forward. A ride that normally took one hour lasted three, but I arrived safely.

Here's what surprised me: Once I changed my driving to match the conditions, I actually enjoyed it. The silence was relaxing and the snow was stunningly beautiful.

Driving safely through a storm requires that you change *how* you drive; you have to stay alert and adapt to the shifting conditions.

Welcome to life. The conditions are constantly shifting—almost as fast and frequently as the weather—and if you keep doing the same things in the rain that you did when it was nice and sunny, you'll crash. You need to change your approach.

Change doesn't mean doing *more* of the same: selling harder, working longer hours, being more aggressive. That won't help. If you're playing basketball and suddenly you find yourself on a football field, using more force to bounce the basketball on the grass doesn't make sense. You need to drop the basketball, pick up a football, and run with it.

And notice, when you're running with the football, are you still using basketball skills and muscles and strategies? Are you thinking and acting like a basketball player on a football field? Or have you truly and fully switched games? Have you become a football player?

If you change your approach, not only can you succeed in this moment, but you have also forever expanded your repertoire of movement. And a wider repertoire of movement makes for a better, more effective, more resilient business, and more capable, happier people.

So often we hear about the importance of being consistent. Let that go. Try to be *inconsistent*. Modify your action to match the changing terrain. Because it's always changing. So there's no simple formula that will get you through every situation you encounter.

Well, except maybe this one.

Before you do or say anything, ask yourself three questions:

1. What's the situation? (The outcome you want to achieve? The risks? The time pressures? The needs?)
2. Who else is involved? (What are their strengths? Weaknesses? Values? Vulnerabilities? Needs?)
3. How can I help? (What are your strengths? Weaknesses? Values? Vulnerabilities?)

Then, and *only* then, decide what you will do or say. Choose the response that leverages your strengths, uses your weaknesses, reflects your differences, expresses your passion, and *meets people where they are and is appropriate to the situation you're in.*

Let's say the economic environment is weak. What's the situation? In an era when huge, established businesses have faltered, the new competitive advantages are trust, reliability, and relationships.

Who else is involved? Think about your clients, prospects, and employees. What are they looking for in this situation? Where are they vulnerable? What support do they need?

Then think about how you can help. What can you offer that will support others *at this time*?

Once you've thought this through in general, apply it in real time when specific opportunities present themselves. For example, let's say a client wants to cancel part of a project he had previously committed to.

You'll have an immediate, instinctive reaction. Maybe you desperately need the money to stay profitable. Maybe you believe that contracts should never be broken.

Maybe you don't trust your client; you think he's taking advantage of you.

But before you act instinctively, *pause*. Take a breath. Ask yourself the three questions. What's the outcome you're trying to achieve? Immediate money? A long-term relationship? Respect in the industry? Something else?

Knowing that trust is the new competitive advantage, you might choose a different response. Maybe you give the client some wiggle room. Which, perhaps, is not your natural, habitual reaction. But you realize it shows understanding, which builds trust and relationships, which, in these economic conditions, is a great investment.

Then you discover something else. A hidden gift in an otherwise depressing economy. Your client put you in a tough spot, and you rose to the occasion, showing true character, which created a deeper relationship. When the economy improves, chances are you've got a client for life. A devoted fan, maybe even a friend, who will refer you to many other clients, because you took a chance for him.

This is the interesting part: That opportunity would never have presented itself if the economy hadn't turned bad, if the client hadn't needed a favor, and if you hadn't paused, understood the opportunity, and taken a chance.

Value investors will tell you that they make all their money when the market is depressed. That gives them the opportunity to buy low. Think of any obstacle as the equivalent of buying low. A poor economy is an opportunity to forge relationships that will last for decades. A failure is the opportunity to rectify the mistake and develop deep, committed, loyal employees, customers, and partners.

Change isn't a distraction. It's not an impediment. It doesn't need to slow you down. Think of it as an opportunity to show your flexibility and build trust as a consequence.

Pause. Breathe. Ask the three questions. Who knows, it's possible you might even find some beauty in a storm.

Stay alert and adapt to changing situations. Keep your eye on the ball, whichever ball that may be.

Where We Are

Mastering yourself. Following through on your ideas and commitments. Knowing when a distraction is useful and when it's an obstacle. Knowing when you're trying to be too perfect or too focused or too productive.

In the right doses, these things can be useful. In the wrong doses, they get in the way. And if you're having a hard time following through, that's a good sign they might be working against you. Doing things half right, imperfectly, flexibly, and with a certain amount of healthy distraction might be just the solution to keeping you on track and moving forward.

Where We've Landed

In part 1, you set yourself up for success by seeing yourself clearly, being willing to question yourself, and being prepared to pause and focus on the outcome you want.

In part 2, you combined your strengths, weaknesses, differences, and passions to uncover your sweet spot for success and happiness. After becoming aware of a few pitfalls that might get in your way, you homed in on the five or so things around which you can focus your year.

In part 3, you took those five things and created a template for a daily to-do list that will keep you moving in the direction you want to go. Using the 18-minute plan, that to-do list, and your calendar, you're keeping yourself on track each day, observing what works and shifting when necessary.

In part 4, you learned that sometimes distractions can be useful. But when they're not, you acquired a series of tools—some words, some actions, some thoughts—to vanquish them. Enabling you to master your initiative, master your boundaries, and master yourself in the service of your annual focus.

So now what? Hopefully, you've already incorporated many of these ideas, tools, and techniques into your life and are already feeling their influence. No matter where you are, what's your best next step? It's only one thing.

CONCLUSION

Now What?

46

You Don't Have Ten Gold Behaviors

Choosing Your One Thing

I lost eighteen pounds in a month and a half.

I didn't exercise harder or longer than usual. I didn't read a new diet book supported by evidence and filled with rules and recipes. I didn't go to a trainer.

I've done all those things in the past, and some of them worked, but none of them lasted. They were too complicated or too expensive or too cumbersome to continue.

So I made a different decision this time. A much simpler one.

First, a little background on losing weight. Every new diet book explains why it's better than all the previous ones. This new plan, the author claims with enthusiasm, holds the key to losing weight and keeping it off forever. It will succeed where the others have failed.

So we decrease our fat consumption. Or increase it. We eat more protein. Or less. We raise our intake of carbohydrates. Or reduce it. And the question lingers: Which is the best diet to lose weight?

Well, we now have the answer. A study published in *The New England Journal of Medicine* put 811 overweight adults through four different diets, each one a different proportion of fat, carbohydrates, and protein.

The result? On average, participants lost twelve pounds after six months and kept nine pounds off after two years. *No matter which diet they followed.*

Certainly, some diets are healthier than others. But in terms of losing weight? No diet was better than any other. Because all diets work through a single mechanism—they restrict your calorie intake. People lose weight when they eat less.

If that's true, then the best diet is the simplest one. So I asked myself: What's the one thing I can change that will make the biggest difference in my calorie consumption? Everyone has one thing.

Mine was sugar. Sometimes I would eat three bowls of ice cream in a day. If I changed that, everything else would work itself out. Cutting out sugar was the one thing that would give me the highest return.

So I stopped eating it. No more cookies, candy, cake, ice cream. That's the only change I consciously made. I sidestepped millions of complex little decisions that most diets require—counting, weighing, choosing, deciding. No phases, no recipes, no thinking.

Each person's one thing could be different. For some, it

might be fried foods. For others, meat. For others still, soft drinks. What's important is to keep it simple.

The implications of this are huge, not just for diets but for all behavior change. After all, what else is a diet but behavior change?

Typically, people overwhelm themselves with tasks in their eagerness to make a change successfully. But that's a mistake. Instead, they should take the time up front to figure out the one and only thing that will have the highest impact and then focus 100 percent of their effort on that one thing.

You've just finished this book and no doubt have lots of great ideas about what you could do differently. Over time you can implement many of them. Maybe you already have. If you're having difficulty starting, though, choose your one thing—the one thing that will make the biggest impact.

Maybe it's structuring your to-do list around your annual focus. Maybe it's stopping multitasking. Or maybe, it's pausing every hour to take a deep breath and refocus.

Choose the one thing that you think—given your particular situation—will make the biggest difference in your life. Choose it and do it.

After that, you can begin to incorporate more aspects of the plan. In fact, they'll probably start to incorporate themselves.

Once I stopped eating sugar, I began to do other things—like exercise more routinely and eat more vegetables and less fat. I didn't force myself to do those things. They just seemed to happen once I started avoiding sugar.

A few years ago, a *Fortune* 100 client asked me to design a new leadership training program. They already had one and had spent several years training people in it, but now they wanted a new one. Why? Because the current one wasn't having the impact they wanted.

I asked to see the old one. Honestly? While I'd love to say my leadership ideas are far superior, I thought the ones they were using were equally good. Leadership models are no different from diets—most of them are just fine. The brilliance is rarely in the model; it's in the implementation.

Don't start from scratch, I pleaded with them. You've already spent years spreading the word, inculcating the language, and socializing the concepts of the old leadership methodology. People are familiar with it. Don't get rid of it.

Just simplify it. Reduce it to its essence. What's the one thing that will have the greatest impact on your leadership?

After some thought, they concluded that if managers communicated more with their employees, it would solve the majority of their issues. Great, I suggested, focus all your efforts on that. Let everything else go.

Brandon, a friend of mine, called me, disheartened, after his business didn't work out. He decided to take a few months off before starting his next venture, and we discussed how he should spend his time. It turns out that Brandon is dyslexic and has always had difficulty reading.

We agreed he should do one thing in his time off: Read every day. That's unusual advice from me. Usually, I tell people to forget about their weaknesses and focus on their strengths. But in Brandon's case the dividend will be huge. If he can tackle reading, not only will it open doors for him, but he'll also conquer the one thing he thought he couldn't do. That confidence will change everything else in his life.

If you're going to work on a weakness, always choose a single, high-leverage one.

A large retail chain with stores all over the world developed ten "Gold" behaviors they wanted all sales associates to exhibit. Things like greet each customer, ask customers if they want an accessory at the point of sale, measure customers for a good fit, and thank each customer for shopping at the store. Stores in which sales associates exhibited all ten behaviors saw a substantial increase in sales.

After some time, the corporate office sent in mystery shoppers to see how the sales associates were doing. Management was pleased: On average, the associates were displaying nine of the ten behaviors.

I asked the project lead if they had seen a change in sales as a result of this 90 percent success rate. After a short inspection of the data, it turned out they hadn't.

So we looked to see if the associates were each missing different behaviors or if they were avoiding a specific one of the ten. As we suspected, they were all skipping the same behavior: measuring customers for a good fit. Which means the other nine behaviors—the ones they were already performing—were immaterial since they didn't impact sales.

"You don't have ten Gold behaviors," I told the project lead, "you have one. Measuring customers for a good fit is your one thing." That was the one thing the salespeople could do differently to make more sales. We instructed the sales associates to focus solely on doing that one thing. Sales shot up.

Choose the one thing you've read from this book that will make the most difference in your life and do it. No matter what. Then, naturally, you will start to incorporate others. And, with time, you'll find that your life moves in a purposeful direction.

Because the moments add up to days, the days add up to years, and the years add up to your life. Making sure that your days and moments are guided by what you want to accomplish with your years means each moment will reflect the life you choose to live. So you'll know you're getting the right things done.

It all starts with your one thing.

Acknowledgments

Some say that writing is a lonely endeavor. That has not been my experience. This book has many fingerprints on it, and I am thankful for them all.

I am lucky enough to have found the kind of advocate that writers dream about in Rick Wolff, my publisher and editor. Thank you—and your team at Business Plus—for your enthusiasm for this book, your vision of how to bring it together, and your unrelenting support of my ideas.

Giles Anderson, you are exactly the agent I wished for. Thank you for finding Rick, and for your reliability, your integrity, and your commitment. You're a magnificent collaborator.

Katherine Bell, my editor at *Harvard Business Review*, thank you for being such a tremendous editor and encouraging partner, for believing in me, for creating space for my voice, and for caring about stories and the very personal side of leadership. Daisy Wademan, thank you for your generous spirit. Without you, my writing would still be sitting on my computer.

I am surrounded by many friends whose editing suggestions continue to shape my own writing. Mermer Blakeslee, thank you for more than thirty years of coaching; it's just beginning to stick. I'm inspired by your voice and so appreciate the way you help me strengthen mine. Anthony Bregman, Howie Jacobson, and Eleanor, thank you for reading my pieces and having something to say about each one that makes it better. Your opinions mean a great deal to me (even in those instances when I don't follow your advice). Esther DeCambra, thank you for your impressive insights and for giving up your life for two weeks. Betsy Inglesby, thank you, for your special affinity, for commas. Stacy Bass, thank you for your artistic eye and, together with Howie, your irrepressible enthusiasm. You guys inspire me. Paul Burger, thank you for your sage advice and for having my back; you deserve to be paid more. Jessica Gelson, thank you for being such a champion of my writing (and me).

Thank you to my clients who are so often my source of inspiration. I am so appreciative of your willingness to be a part of my stories, and I never take for granted the trust you put in me. Thank you to the readers of my blog; your presence, comments, and emails keep me going. Thank you to GNOWP, to Bavli Yerushalmi, to the Rosenfields and the Bakers, and to my family—Anthony and Malaika, Bertie and Rachel, Robbie, Susan (your love is still so clearly with us), Catherine, and Margaret Harrison, Jerry and Margaret

Wolfe, and all the Weintraubs; your words of encourage-
ment and caring criticism energize me and offer me invaluable guidance.

Mama and Papa, thank you for believing in me, loving
me, growing with me, and supporting me. Always.

Isabelle, Sophia, and Daniel, you are such brilliant lights
in my life. Thank you for your love, your laughter, your joy,
your sadness, and even your anger. Thank you for being so
fully yourselves.

And Eleanor, my love, I could not invent a more perfect
partner. Thank you for loving me for who I am while
encouraging me to grow. I thank God every day that we
are traveling this life together. You make me a better person. You make it easy to take risks.

INDEX

ABOUT THE AUTHOR

Peter Bregman advises and consults with CEOs and their leadership teams in organizations ranging from *Fortune* 500 companies to start-ups to nonprofits. He speaks worldwide on how people can lead, work, and live more powerfully. He is a frequent guest on public radio, provides commentary for CNN, and writes for *Harvard Business Review, Fast Company, Forbes*, and *Psychology Today*. Peter lives in New York City and can be reached at www.peter bregman.com.

To download an *18 Minutes* template and get other helpful resources go to www.peterbregman.com/18.